Culture is Everything

How to Become a True Culture Warrior and Lead Your Organization to Victory

Coming soon from Quality Press

Connected, Intelligent, Automated: The Definitive Guide to Digital Transformation and Quality 4.0
Nicole Radziwill

Climbing the Curve of Quality and Continuous Improvement: Lessons from Psychology and Behavioral Economics
Debashis Sarkar

Other culture titles from Quality Press

Unleash Quality: Building a Winning Strategy for a Culture of Quality That Will Unleash Your Growth and Profit Potential
Arron S. Angle

We Move Our Own Cheese! A Business Fable About Championing Change
Victor E. Sower and Frank K. Fair

Other management titles from Quality Press

The Journey: Achieving Sustained Organizational Success
Charles A. Cianfrani, Isaac Sheps, and John E. (Jack) West

Senior Management and Quality: How to Leverage Quality for Profit
Fin Rooney

New from Quality Press

Data Quality: Dimensions, Measurement, Strategy, Management, and Governance
Rupa Mahanti

A Practical Field Guide for ISO 13485:2016: Medical Devices—Quality Management Systems—Requirements for Regulatory Purposes
Erik V. Myhrberg and Joseph Raciti, with Brandon L. Myhrberg

Data Integrity and Compliance: A Primer for Medical Product Manufacturers
José Rodríguez-Pérez

Root Cause Analysis, Second Edition: The Core of Problem Solving and Corrective Action
Duke Okes

For more information on Quality Press titles, please visit our website at: http://www.asq.org/quality-press

Culture is Everything

How to Become a True Culture Warrior and
Lead Your Organization to Victory

Jeff Veyera

ASQ

Quality Press
Milwaukee, Wisconsin

American Society for Quality, Quality Press, Milwaukee 53203
© 2020 by Jeffrey A. Veyera
All rights reserved. Published 2020
Printed in the United States of America
23 22 21 20   5 4 3 2 1

Publisher's Cataloging-in-Publication Data

Names: Veyera, Jeff, author.
Title: Culture is Everything : How to Become a True Culture Warrior and Lead Your Organization to Victory / Jeff Veyera.
Description: Includes bibliographical references. | Milwaukee, WI: Quality Press, 2020.
Identifiers: LCCN: 2019056787 | ISBN: 978-1-951058-03-6 (pbk.) | 978-1-951058-04-3 (epub) | 978-1-951058-05-0 (pdf)
Subjects: LCSH Corporate culture. | Leadership. | Success in business. | Organizational change. | Organizational learning. | BISAC BUSINESS & ECONOMICS / Leadership | BUSINESS & ECONOMICS / Organizational Behavior | BUSINESS & ECONOMICS / Workplace Culture | BUSINESS & ECONOMICS / Quality Control
Classification: LCC HD57.7 .V48 2020 | DDC 658.4—dc23

ISBN: 978-1-915058-03-6 (Spiralbound)
ISBN: 978-951058-04-3 (EPUB)
ISBN: 978-1-951058-05-0 (PDF)

Publisher: Seiche Sanders
Managing Editor: Sharon Woodhouse
Sr. Creative Services Specialist: Randy L. Benson

ASQ Mission: The American Society for Quality advances individual, organizational, and community excellence worldwide through learning, quality improvement, and knowledge exchange.

Attention Bookstores, Wholesalers, Schools, and Corporations: Quality Press books, video, audio, and software are available at quantity discounts with bulk purchases for business, educational, or instructional use. For information, please contact Quality Press at 800-248-1946, or write to Quality Press, P.O. Box 3005, Milwaukee, WI 53201-3005.

To place orders or to request a free copy of the ASQ Quality Press Publications Catalog, visit our website at http://www.asq.org/quality-press.

 Printed on acid-free paper.

Quality Press
600 N. Plankinton Ave.
Milwaukee, WI 53203-2914
Email: books@asq.org

ASQ Excellence Through Quality™

For Anita, who has heard all these stories already—four times.

TABLE OF CONTENTS

Culture Is Everything

Does that sound like hyperbole? Perhaps it strikes the ear in such a manner as to make you wonder whether the author has gotten carried away with monographic myopia. How can culture be *all* that matters in business?

Sure, we've all heard that "culture eats strategy for breakfast." But doesn't that merely mean that certain kinds of strategy better match certain cultures than others? For example, we wouldn't expect stodgy old buttoned-down GE to successfully drive the same strategies that a hot Silicon Valley startup would, right? Old dogs don't learn new tricks very easily.

And yes, we certainly must admit that company culture is the topic of some discussion at present, in no small part because those tech sector disruptors like Amazon simply will not shut up about the cultures they've built and how important these are to their ongoing success. Culture is cool. But is it everything?

Surely there are many other factors which are more predictive of a company's long-term success than its culture. In *Good to Great* and its sequels, for example, Jim Collins emphasizes the importance of leadership. A top leader (Level 5 in his terminology) is often the difference maker in separating the truly special companies from the rest of the pack. Isn't superior leadership a significant driver of company performance?[1]

Luck must count somewhere as well. Isn't that the real difference between MySpace and Facebook, when you think about it? Betamax was the technically superior technology to VHS; it failed due to poor luck. It doesn't matter how much fun your teammates are having if you get snake-bitten by events. As Nassim Nicholas Taleb persuasively argues, "black swan" events do occur, are quite difficult to predict in advance, and can be extremely disruptive.[2] Take the financial crisis in 2008 as but one example. Fortune favors the bold, but misfortune can strike anybody.

Let's face it—government picks winners and losers in the marketplace all the time. That's why there are so many lobbyists. The State doesn't give a fig about how well you do on employee engagement surveys. It cares about compliance with regulations, the avoidance of antitrust concerns, the company's ability to provide jobs, and the millions of dollars in tax revenue associated with the firm. If your company is a heavy hitter and that scrappy startup with the game-changing technology threatens it, the bureaucracy will build those barriers to entry higher and save your market share. You can build a better mousetrap, but it's government that decides whether the world can beat a path to your door—because it builds the roads. Shouldn't government favor, therefore, matter more than what company leadership tacks to the walls?

Besides, if culture truly were everything, all these companies with horrible cultures getting panned on Glassdoor.com would be consigned to the scrap heap. Those in the Quality and Lean trenches know that there are far more awful cultures out there than great ones, and yet we still somehow get the job done, right?

In the following pages, I will convince you that culture *is* everything and rebut these arguments definitively in the process. Moreover, I will demonstrate to you that efforts undertaken without regard to company culture are doomed to irrelevance if not outright failure; that it is folly to state (as we in the Lean community in particular are wont to do) that having a certain kind of culture is a prerequisite for our approach to continuous improvement to work, and then make no effort to determine whether that requirement has been met; and that in certain cases, you will have no choice but to either transform the company culture or relinquish the goal. Finally, I will provide you with a toolkit to help you navigate the battlefields of the corporate culture wars and thereby maximize your chances of survival. And don't worry: along the way I'll pepper the text with the war stories upon which a lifetime of reflection finally convinced me, every bit as skeptical as you, that culture is in fact everything in business success. As Mary Poppins sang, *A spoonful of sugar helps the medicine go down.*

Let's begin.

ONE

What Is a Company Culture?

"It seems like those of us who run a business can't go five minutes without encountering the term 'company culture.' The phrase is always uttered with extreme adoration, yet the very concept seems as nebulous as it is elusive."

—LEAH BUSQUE[3]

Nebulous and Elusive

That sort of fuzzy terminology doesn't bode well for a book about company culture, particularly for an audience that will likely be comprised largely of hard-nosed engineers and business leaders who have built their entire careers on precision and attention to detail.

Let's lift some of this fog right from the jump: A company's culture exists to help the company achieve its objectives. There is no other reason for it to exist. If you work for the English football club Manchester United, you are there for one reason and one reason only—to win the championship. Every aspect of the organization's culture is defined through this one objective. Anything taking focus off this objective, no matter how otherwise desirable it might be, is necessarily countercultural and requires additional effort to happen. Were you to propose, for example, that the team hire a talentless-but-lovable teen idol as goalkeeper because it would boost interest in the club by teenage girls, you could expect considerable resistance due to cultural misalignment.

The first service I shall do the reader in this book is to dispel the miasma that suffuses the very concept of company culture by proposing a definition, which, within the covers of this work if nowhere else, will allow us to properly explore the topic in useful breadth and depth. To whit: Company culture is the manner by which an organization's values are communicated, understood, and lived by its members.

Let's unpack that definition a bit. It's important.

"The manner"—A culture is a living thing; it involves motion and action. It is a way of doing something. When we speak of American culture or French culture or Ancient Egyptian culture, we may think immediately of cultural artifacts (movies or paintings or pyramids), but those artifacts were created in order to do something of value to the creator or his or her patron. Similarly, a company culture does not exist because people need something to do to kill time, but rather because the company needs to do something in order to achieve its goals.

"Organization's values"—Why values? Why not goals, or strategy, or metrics, or hiring practices, and so on? Because culture is upstream of goals, strategy, metrics, and hiring practices. For example, if your company highly prizes integrity and ethical behavior, it will not pursue opportunities or means of achieving them that conflict with these values. Culture takes some potential actions off the table as values filter the universe of possible behaviors and actions down to those which are acceptable for the culture being built. When football fans speak of "The Patriot Way," they often invoke the cultural value of personal accountability (in the form of "do your job"). This is such a dearly held value that in the barrage of postgame interviews you will not hear New England's players or coaches making excuses, blaming others, or even saying, "That's not my job." To do so would be to betray the organization in a fundamental manner and guarantee a one-way ticket out of Gillette Stadium. The offender would be exposed as not sharing the team's values, a crime which cannot be tolerated in any winning outfit.

"Communicated, understood, and lived"—As we'll soon demonstrate, what we call a company's culture can be quite different depending on whether we are referring to what has been said, what has been comprehended, or what has been done. Few companies lack some provision in their list of values for ethical considerations, and yet examples are legion of high-ranking employees failing to understand how to behave in a manner that will not land the company in court. Even where the values are backed up by policy and procedural guidance, actual practice can be quite different. To define a company's culture, then, it stands to reason that all three areas need to be examined. In the end, it is how the culture is lived which will determine how successful goals, strategy, and the rest will be, springing as they do from the cultural values.

"By its members"—Note that this includes all of the organization's members, not just the executive leadership team or the customer-facing teammates. Culture is carried like genetic code by each and every person within the company. If we claim to have a customer-focused culture but our call center personnel are foul tempered and rude, the customer will see a very different set of norms as typical of our organization, and our brilliant marketing strategy to brand ourselves as The Customer Care Colossus will fail miserably. It extends beyond customer-facing employees too—we may pride ourselves on integrity yet look the other way when Ted from IT uses the company cloud drive to store his photos from his Sumatran vacation last summer. At least one company I know of prided itself on its commitment to its employees yet reserved a bunch of parking places by name for its company officers, very few of whom even lived in the same state where the headquarters were located. As George Orwell famously put it in *Animal Farm*, "All animals are equal. But some animals are more equal than others."[4]

This definition of company culture is illustrated by the following diagram.

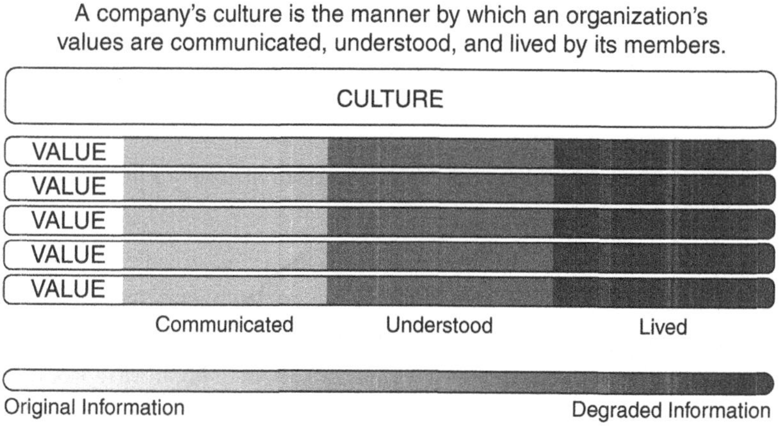

A company's culture is the manner by which an organization's values are communicated, understood, and lived by its members.

FIGURE 1. Company culture definition

There can be a wide discrepancy between desired values and practiced values due to the miscommunication, misunderstanding, or misapplication of these values. This has the effect of attenuating the information being conveyed from the leadership of the company and compromising the company's ability to attain its objectives.

An analogy underscores this point.[5] Napoleon Bonaparte, emperor of the French, revolutionized warfare in his day by the ease with which he split his forces and swiftly marched them, often appearing on the battlefield before his coalition opponents could join their forces and defeating their forces in turn. Key to this remarkable military capability was Bonaparte's standing order to his generals: "March to the sound of the guns." In an age when issuing orders to one's subordinate commanders meant writing them out on paper and sending them via messenger on horseback, the timeliness of the order was always suspect. Situations often greatly changed on the battlefield during the time it took to transmit the order. "March to the sound of the guns" allowed commanders who were following outdated instructions to recover and have an impact on the battlefield, perhaps providing the margin of victory.

At Waterloo, a newly minted marshal named Emmanuel de Grouchy was ordered to pursue the Prussian Army and prevent its combination with its British allies. Grouchy couldn't catch up with the fleeing Prussians by the time the battle of Waterloo began. When he heard the guns firing, he didn't do what was required of a marshal of France under that Napoleonic military culture. He kept to his original orders, eventually defeating a single Prussian corps at the battle of Wavre, but by this time Napoleon had already been vanquished by the combined might of the British and Prussians at Waterloo. The failure of one man to live out the culture as communicated and understood in this instance changed the course of history and the fate of nations. Imagine what such a failure can do to your company!

We change agents continually swim with or against company cultures. In some companies, on some teams, at times, our work is relatively easy and extremely fun. If we're training others, we achieve engagement almost effortlessly due to their natural interest in what we're trying to teach them to do. If we're working on a project, our colleagues shoulder their burdens cheerfully, and we progress steadily from ideation through implementation. If we're coaching others, we can see them grow and blossom as they apply our advice to seize the opportunities spotted. We have the Midas touch; every project we touch turns to gold. Occasionally we speak at industry conferences, not simply to share our wisdom and perhaps teach others how to enjoy some small modicum of the success we have had, but also to spend breaks and happy hours basking in the endless chorus of "I wish my job were half as fulfilling as yours!" and "How did you ever find this opportunity?"[6] As drinks pile up, there will even be a "Wish I had your luck" or three, but who cares when you're having the time of your professional life? "Shake it off," as the great quality philosopher Taylor Swift once said.[7]

At other companies, on other teams, at other times, sympathetic colleagues approach us and place their hands on our shoulders saying, "Man, I wouldn't want your job."[8] We're swimming against the cultural tide, trying first and foremost to get people to see something—anything!—that is transparently obvious to us. Eyes roll. Teammates think or even say, "There they go again." E-mails go unread, meetings unattended, timelines extended asymptotically toward infinity. Time and again we leap at The Opportunity—arrived at last!—only to find another mirage. We start going to ASQ (American Society for Quality) meetings simply so we can confirm that it is not us who are crazy, but the cultures with which we contend. We start thinking about easier and more edifying jobs, like mucking out stables or sparring with mixed martial arts championship contenders.

The difference between gigs we'll tell our grandchildren about and those we'll tell our therapists about is down to culture. Culture is everything.

What makes for the kind of company culture that drives process engineers to dance through the hallways like Julie Andrews singing her way across Alpine meadows?[9] We'll address that mystery in the next chapter.

TWO

Dimensions of a Company Culture

"Part of company culture is path-dependent—it's the lessons you learn along the way."

—JEFF BEZOS[10]

If a company's culture is the manner by which an organization's values are communicated, understood, and lived by its members, what are its essential elements? What are the mechanisms by which culture transmits these values?

Let's begin our examination with a very common facet of company cultures every quality professional has run into. How many times while preparing for a process improvement engagement have you heard the following from a senior stakeholder: "Sure, we have documentation, but nobody follows it. Everything here is tribal knowledge"? By "tribal knowledge," they mean that essential information regarding how to perform the process is passed along verbally from person to person without recourse to written guidance, generally by demonstrating how it is done and providing some commentary on the finer nuances of the task at hand. This means that promulgating process improvements will require extensive missionary work in this culture, as one cannot simply rely on teammates to faithfully follow an updated procedure—they're not a "by the book" kind of operation.

This provides a useful window into the dynamics of how different cultures operate. Let's imagine there are two kinds of company cultures: one which is exclusively "tribal knowledge," where nothing is written down; one which is "by the book," where the process is rigidly controlled by the applicable procedure. Every other company's culture necessarily falls between these two polar opposites, as seen in Figure 2.

WHAT DEFINES HOW PROCESSES ARE PERFORMED?

Common Practice	Documented Standards
aka "Tribal Knowledge"	aka "By the Book"

FIGURE 2. Example of a dimension

To the left we see Common Practice, which we might also call "tribal knowledge" or "custom." This represents the reality in some companies that the floor is essentially run based upon tradition. An auditor would spot this by the absence or ignorance of documented work instructions and mistake-proofing techniques. "This is the way we do things around here" is the rallying cry in such cultures.

We contrast this with the "By the Book" culture at the right and its emphasis on Documented Standards. "We do things by the book around here" is what you might hear as an auditor in such a place, which no doubt would be wallpapered with work instructions if not highly automated (automation is only truly a reality where the process is highly repeatable and very standardized).[11]

In alluding to a hypothetical auditor I've tipped my hand to, the next discussion topic associated with cultural dimensions is: How do you know where you fall on a spectrum like this? After all, we've stated that many companies will fall somewhere in between the extremes of any dimension. How do we determine where?

To evaluate where a given culture fits along a spectrum, we have to observe the behavior of the people in that culture. The sample quotes I've provided above are one indicator. The existence or lack of standards displayed in the workplace are another. Where standards do exist but are not being followed, we could observe key points of the standard and use standard compliance as a proxy for this question of authority. We could conduct an experiment, releasing the next version of a standard and having an influential employee deviate from it, then track what proportion of the team hews to the standard and which does not.

For the sake of simplicity and getting started on evaluating your culture, however, let's leverage a best practice from a risk management tool called Failure Mode and Effects Analysis (FMEA) and apply objective scales based on common practices in cultures at each end of the spectrum, as seen in Figure 3 below.

An objective scale such as this one can be created for any cultural dimension of interest. The numerical rating allows us to quantify results. Having five ratings allows us to stratify these results in a meaningful way that a high/low scale would not, while still keeping evaluation simple enough that we will not have to

Rating	Criteria
5	Standards are prominently displayed for all significant tasks, and compliance is 80%+ OR process mistake-proofed so that deviation from standard is not possible.
4	Documented standards are prominently displayed for all significant tasks, but compliance is 80% or less with these standards.
3	Documented standards are prominently displayed for all significant tasks, but compliance is 50% or less with these standards.
2	Documented standards exist but are neither displayed nor deliberately followed.
1	No evidence of documented standards in workplace.

FIGURE 3. Objective scale for process management dimension

spend endless hours arguing whether a 7.5 or an 8 is more appropriate in a given circumstance.

Now that we've explained the basic approach, it's time to complicate the model a bit (with good reason, as we'll soon see).

In our definition of culture, we distinguish between culture as communicated, as understood, and as lived. This implies that there are in effect at least three types of culture in play in any given organization at any given time.[12] Would not the ratings for these across the various dimensions likely be different? Our conceptual model now looks like Figure 4.

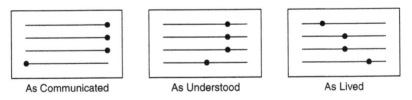

| As Communicated | As Understood | As Lived |

FIGURE 4. Three lenses on company culture

In the hypothetical example above, the culture in reality is quite different from that communicated by leadership, in part because it wasn't understood perfectly by teammates. While the culture as lived is no doubt the most important cultural lens from the perspective of process improvement efforts, we need to consider what has been communicated and understood when either reforming or transforming company culture. More on that later.

Cultural dimensions will be the same even where the ratings for As Communicated, As Understood, and As Lived are different. But what are these dimensions?

There are many potential buckets in which we could place aspects of company culture. As our primary concern from a business process improvement perspective is generally limited to how a company is steered and how a company views change, we will begin our investigation there. With regard to how a company is guided, consider a simple spectrum from control by a few decision makers (this may be typical of a small family business) to many decision makers (think of a Silicon Valley tech company with lots of subject matter experts filling different niches). In terms of how the company views change, posit for the moment that this spectrum runs from a strong preference for preserving the

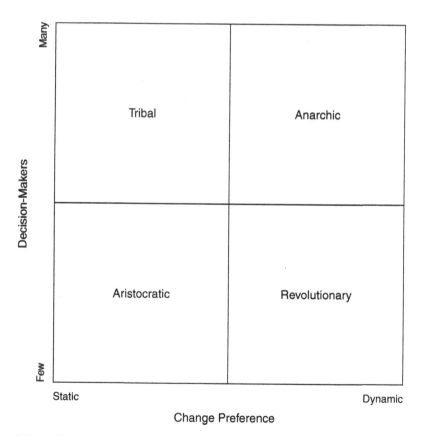

FIGURE 5. Cultural type 4-blocker

status quo (or perhaps even reclaiming past glory) we'll deem "static" (a long-standing, traditional company), to one with an irresistible attraction to disruption (a scrappy startup) that we'll call "dynamic." Please note this is the general standing of the company taken as a whole; there will always be individuals with opposing preferences.

In our example definition at the top of the chapter, we discussed "tribal knowledge" cultures. In Figure 5, we can see more clearly where that concept comes from: it is typical in companies where decision-making is highly decentralized and where there is a preference for preserving the status quo. Teammates in these tribes tend to resist efforts to implement documented process standards because it represents a loss of their authority, which they wish to preserve, in addition to a change from the way in which work is done at present. By contrast, teammates in a "revolutionary" culture tend to resist documented standards as being too inflexible, although they may welcome the idea of an elite few defining them and guiding the many in how they work. The main appeal of standards will be in "aristocratic" cultures, where the combination of control and slowing down change may be irresistible; imposing such standards will fail miserably in an "anarchic" environment as the tendency to buck against rules while moving at high speed to seize opportunity will carry the day.[13]

While these general categories are useful in helping us understand the general cultural geography, we will need more precision in crafting specific strategies for process improvement and must go one level deeper in our analysis. Consider the tree diagram below.

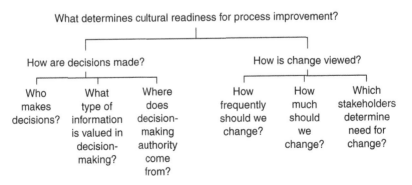

FIGURE 6. Cultural dimensions tree diagram

For each of the questions on the bottom branches of the tree diagram, we could doubtless posit a nearly infinite array of potential responses. More useful would be to envision a spectrum of responses for each, running from two opposite poles within the questions area of discussion:

- Who makes decisions? Few vs. many
- What type of information is valued in decision-making? Qualitative vs. quantitative
- Where does decision-making authority come from? Rank/position vs. credibility/ knowledge
- How frequently should we change? Static vs. dynamic
- How much should we change? Incremental vs. fundamental
- Which stakeholders determine need for change? Internal vs. external

We will now further define useful dimensions of company culture.

It is true that these six are chiefly applicable to the process improvement efforts near and dear to the hearts of an audience comprised chiefly of Quality Improvement and Lean practitioners. They may not be the most important cultural dimensions for other applications. The principle still applies, and other dimensions of interest could be created fairly easily once you're familiar with the rest of the content of this book and have some experience putting this wisdom into practice. For example, "innovation cultures" have become hot topics of conversation of late. You can build fresh templates for the various dimensions of culture that foster greater creativity, and then apply the methods I'll describe to you later on in this book to migrate your company toward this culture once you're familiar with the basic concepts. It is a very flexible approach, one practically begging to be pulled and stretched to the very limit by brilliant and practical people like yourself. Besides, process improvement professionals are tinkerers; we have to play with the toys we're given and find new and exciting ways to get even more out of them than their inventors or discoverers ever anticipated. It's all just a bunch of brightly colored Legos until smart people assemble it into something useful to solve the problems which besiege us.

From these basic building blocks, we will build out our framework for understanding company culture archetypes, define the type of culture your company needs in order to fulfill its vision, and develop the assessment tools needed to determine how far your culture is today from what it needs to be tomorrow. Then

Dimension	Definition
Decision-Makers (DM)	How dispersed decision-making authority regarding process is across the company. Where teammates are very empowered, there will be many decision-makers; where process control is highly centralized, there will be few decision-makers.
Decisive Information (DI)	What type of information is prized and determinative in making decisions within the organization. Numbers-driven cultures will score high for quantitative information; gut-driven cultures will score high for qualitative information. Where both are present, select the type which in the end the decision-maker(s) will use to come to a final conclusion.
Decision Authority (DA)	How decision-making authority is defined. In hierarchical organizations like the military, rank or positional authority determines who decides; in startup companies or virtual organizations, credibility and knowledge will be determinative.
Pace of Change (CP)	How often process change is desired within a company. This will range from static environments where the status quo is to be protected to dynamic workplaces where the status quo is to be disrupted.
Magnitude of Change (CM)	How large a desired change may be and still be supported by most within an organization. This may run from tiny, incremental improvements to fundamental redesigns of how we work. This represents the appetite for change.
Driver of Change (CD)	Where the impetus for change comes from. In externally focused cultures, it comes from outside (usually customer, sometimes market or regulatory). In internally focused cultures, it comes from within the four walls of the company.

FIGURE 7. Cultural dimensions definition

we can employ various ingenious (and occasionally discomfiting) methods to close the gaps between culture as it is today and culture as it could (and should) be tomorrow.

We'll begin by defining some common culture types in light of the dimensions defined in this chapter.

THREE

Company Culture Archetypes

"Customers will never love a company until the
employees love it first."

—SIMON SINEK[14]

There are all sorts of company cultures, just as there are all sorts of people. At the most granular level, every company is different; at the very highest level, every company is the same. In between, we have some useful archetypes we can point to which will help us define company cultures in useful ways along the dimensions previously provided.

Let's see if you can identify some famous company cultures from the following patterns of cultural dimensions:

1. This company's culture features work processes designed by industrial engineers and rigidly enforced to ensure maximum productivity. Numbers are king; careers will be made or broken by metric performance. Authority is hierarchical, both in the C-suite and on the shop floor. Change is frequent and constant; business success often hinges on the smallest efficiencies to be gained. Sweeping change is rare and limited in part by the agreement with the labor union. Change is generally generated internally to seize opportunities, but there are some major disruptors in this industry (who also happen to be partners), which leads to a significant amount of change being driven externally.

2. This company prides itself on collaborative decision-making and encouraging leaders to take reasonable risks. It is relentlessly data driven, and credibility comes from the knowledge of the individual; titles are almost unimportant. Large changes are a constant drumbeat as the company seeks to disrupt every

industry it enters. Change is largely driven by customer need and emerging technology.

3. This company seeks to hire and develop the best managerial decision-makers in the business world. Numbers are everything; indeed, sometimes it runs into issues with managers pushing teams too hard to produce or getting creative in reporting. There are well-established career paths in its far-flung business units; pedigree is important and slots for its corporate leadership programs are very closely held. While smaller process decisions may be made through consensus and collaboration at lower levels, any significant change will require sign-off by the appropriate authorities in the chain of command. Change is fairly common in the work processes, and some experimentation is encouraged, although a high degree of rigor is required before implementing proposed changes. The business changes swiftly, and leaders pride themselves on seizing opportunities no one else sees yet.

Pencils down.

If we were to sketch out the likely results of cultural assessments along the 5-point objective scales for these three companies, the following patterns would be evident.

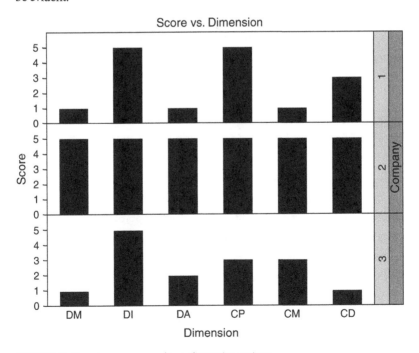

FIGURE 8. Sample company culture dimension ratings

In this comparative view, we can see some differences between these companies, which resemble (but not perfectly) the cultures of UPS, Amazon, and GE. Company 1 is a fairly typical company of the revolutionary bent, featuring tight control and top-down decision-making along with constant tweaking to the process. Company 2 epitomizes the technology startup mentality; empowerment is high (in this case, more so on the development than the operational side of the business), as is the appetite for change. Company 3 is somewhat in the middle of the other two, featuring a hierarchical structure with some room for innovation at the shop-floor level.

With this concept firmly in mind, we'll now propose some archetypes based on these dimensions. It may help to try to identify companies that may epitomize each. You will find a full list of 64 subcategories in Appendix C, but for our primary purpose, we'll discuss only the most relevant archetypes to business process improvement here.

- **Anarchic**—a culture with extremely decentralized decision-making and constant, significant change; akin to a brand new startup.
- **Aristocratic**—a culture at the opposite end of Anarchic in each dimension; distinguished by a strong hierarchy with a strong traditional bent and highly resistant to change.
- **Compliant**—a culture where change happens slowly, but it occurs in an orderly fashion when it does—and tends toward sweeping change on these occasions.
- **Engineering**—a culture which is designed and redesigned based on the expertise of an elite few.
- **Lean**—a culture in which everyone plays a part in incremental improvement of the company.
- **Operations**—a culture that is a meritocracy, based chiefly on the technical competency and ability to drive results of the members—resistant to change but very focused on customer (and sometimes regulatory) requirements.
- **Revolutionary**—a culture undergoing large amounts of change driven by an elite.
- **Six Sigma**—a culture featuring strong leadership control combined with continuous incremental improvement driven by data.
- **Tribalist**—a culture which is both loosely controlled (lots of tribes and chiefs) and highly resistant to change.

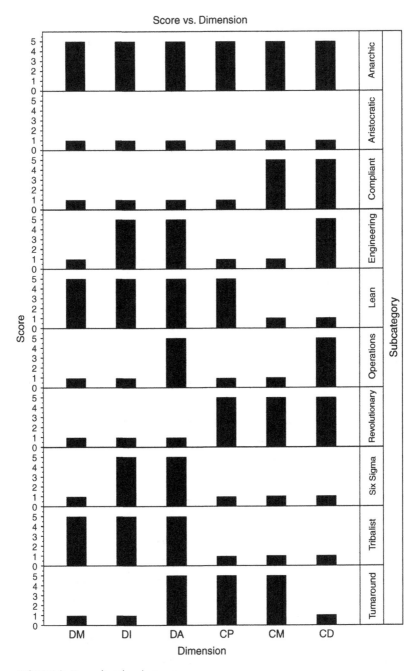

FIGURE 9. Key cultural archetypes

- **Turnaround**—a culture which is internally focused, undergoing frequent, substantial change, guided by a few insiders.

These 10 archetypes represent the most relevant cultures to the success or failure of a business process improvement effort. Please note that different business process improvement methods align best with different archetypes; this is a key principle that will guide our efforts to develop sound strategies in the chapters to come.

While the labels for each archetype are meant to be indicative of the type of leader who thrives in each culture, they lack the precision of legal terms and should not be taken as completely determinative. Nor does it mean that certain business process improvement approaches will never succeed in a hostile culture; merely that certain approaches go with the cultural grain and will have a greater likelihood of success as a result.

Let's kick the tires a bit on this model and see how well it comports to business reality.

You're a Lean expert hired on as an Operations VP for a division of a large, complex company which has struggled with increasing costs and pressure on profit margins. Your mandate is to reduce waste throughout your division and thus reduce cost and increase profits. On your first day, you get the lay of the land from your boss and colleagues. They describe the culture thusly:

- "We like leaders who fit in around here. Don't get out too far ahead of your boss. It is a lot better to ask permission rather than forgiveness."
- "Most of us have been around this business a long time. There's an art to it. Numbers won't tell you what's really going on; you need to ask someone in the know."
- "Your predecessor tried to get another division to adopt her way of handling customer complaints without going through her boss first. That's why you're here now."
- "This isn't rocket science. We work best when we do the same thing every day. Don't rock the boat."
- "Our competitors are eating us for lunch. If we don't do something—and soon—we'll all be in the unemployment line."
- "We won't change a thing unless a customer demands we do."

Based on this smorgasbord of expert commentary, how would you characterize this company in terms of the dimensions we've been discussing?

- Are there many or few real decision-makers?
- Does qualitative or quantitative data carry the day when making decisions?
- Does authority flow from one's position or one's knowledge?
- Is this a static or dynamic company?
- Is there a small or large appetite for change?
- Does the impetus for change come from within or from without the four walls of the company?
- What archetype does this company represent?

If your mapping matches mine, you'll have identified this company as having a Compliant culture. How does that compare with the Lean culture of your dreams? Will this be an easy or a tough job? (We'll leave these last questions for you to ponder).

We have now laid the foundation and introduced the core concepts that will undergird much more detailed discussion to come. We will return again and again to these archetypes; it would be wise to bookmark this section, as you may want to refer back to it as we continue to explore this subject.

One word of caution to the quibblers among us (and the author is a proud quibbler himself; no criticism is implied): If you're an expert in one or more of the cultural archetypes defined in this chapter and you take exception to how they've been characterized, you have full permission and authority to change them to suit your own needs. Humans are biased creatures with limited perceptions; my definitions are not infallibly proclaimed, and you'll get no argument from me if you think a Six Sigma culture ought to be one without gatekeepers and majority opinion ought to rule. We are collaborators, you and I, and if a different formulation helps you to accomplish what you set out to do, you can rest assured that I'll be cheering you on all the way. It is the foolish tailor who dogmatically refuses to cuff the trousers of short-legged men.

But first, let's figure out what kind of culture will suit you best.

FOUR

What Type of Culture Does Your Company Need?

"I think as a company, if you can get those two things right—having a clear direction on what you are trying to do and bringing in great people who can execute on the stuff—then you can do pretty well."

—MARK ZUCKERBERG[15]

Company culture serves a purpose. In a one-person firm, culture is irrelevant: one person does it all, so the company culture is simply however that person chooses to do things. Of course, even so simple a company culture as this can be ill suited for marketplace success. If I am a consultant with a client I'm serving in Bangalore, India, while I live in Los Angeles, California, insisting on keeping to working hours during the time zone my office is found within wouldn't be wise. Nor would rigidly holding to American cultural norms for professional interactions. Not all company cultures set us up for success in those areas necessary for our business to thrive.

As we focus more narrowly on those cultures which align most strongly with process improvement, this becomes clearer still. Companies that were founded by the more autocratic among us will struggle with the very notion of empowerment so necessary to building a strong quality culture. One of the reasons why Toyota has been able to be so fearless in its sharing of the Toyota Production System and Lean approaches is that so few other companies have proven willing to embrace the culture that makes such systems so productive, beginning with the assurance given to employees that they will not lose their jobs due to increasing productivity.[16] Toyota followed W. Edward Deming's call to drive out fear from the workplace as a necessary predicate for true quality improvement; few other companies have been willing to do the same.

This tension between the culture our company needs and the culture it has is a prime driver of transformation and reengineering efforts, which are usually triggered once the market has rejected the company's business model. McKinsey & Company and other management consulting firms enjoy robust business transformation service offerings, which begin with the transplantation of a more successful company culture for this reason. Yet according to McKinsey, 70% of business transformation efforts will fail, despite their success being essential to survival.[17]

What Makes for a Quality Culture?

The undisputed sacred text of the quality professional is Juran's *Quality Handbook*. The sixth edition had this to say about desirable aspects of a company culture vis-à-vis process improvement.

"Some of the more enabling norms are as follows:

A *belief that the quality of a product or process is at least of equal importance, and probably of greater importance, than the mere quantity produced.* This belief results in decisions favoring quality: defective items do not get passed on down the line or out the door; chronic errors and delays are corrected.

A *fanatical commitment to meeting customer needs.* Everyone knows who his or her customers are (those who receive the results of their work), and how well he or she is doing at meeting those needs. (They ask.) Organization members, if necessary, drop everything and go out of their way to assist customers in need.

A *fanatical commitment to stretch goals and continuous improvement.* There is always an economic opportunity for improving products or processes. Organizations who practice continuous improvement keep up with, or become better than, competitors. . . .

A *customer-oriented code of conduct and code of ethics.* This code is published, taught in new employee orientations, and taken into consideration in performance ratings and in distributing rewards. Everyone is expected at all times to behave and make decisions in accordance with the code. The code is enforced, if needed, by managers at all levels. The code applies to everyone, even board members—perhaps especially to them considering their power to influence everyone else.

A belief in continuous adaptive change is not only good but necessary. To remain alive, organizations must develop a system for discovering social, governmental, international, or technological trends that could impact the organization. In addition, organizations will need to create and to maintain structures and processes that enable a quick, effective response to these newly-discovered trends."[18]

Michael L. George described the cultural fertile ground for Six Sigma in his book *Lean Six Sigma*:

"**Customer centricity:** The knowledge of what the customer values most is the start of value stream analysis.

Financial results: No project or effort is undertaken unless there is evidence indicating how much shareholder value will be created. The goal is for each black belt to deliver an average of $500,000 of improved operating profit per year.

Management engagement: The CEO, executives, and managers are *engaged* in Six Sigma. They have designated responsibilities for overseeing and guiding Six Sigma projects to make sure those projects stay focused on organizational priorities.

Resource commitment: A significant number, typically 1% to 3% of the organization's staff, is devoted to Six Sigma efforts full-time and other employees are expected to participate regularly on projects.

Execution infrastructure: The hierarchy of specific roles (such as black belts and master black belts) provides ways to integrate Six Sigma projects into the 'real work' of the organization and sustain the rate of improvement."[19]

Lean practitioners are particularly interested in the cultural foundations for process improvement. *The Lean Handbook* (edited by Anthony Manos and Chad

Vincent) identifies both basic principles necessary to undertake a Lean journey as well as more advanced principles required to sustain a Lean culture:

> "Basic principles: safety, standards, leadership, empowerment, and collaboration.
>
> Advanced principles: systemic thinking, constancy of purpose, social responsibility."[20]

While there are similarities in the cultural recipes articulated above, there are also stark differences. Beyond the general dimensions defined in Chapter 2, additional and more specific dimensions will need to be defined in order to enable the specific methodologies for process improvement to be deployed. Attempting to roll out Lean Six Sigma without standardized work will prove to be an exercise in frustration. Additional dimensions and objective scales are provided in Appendix B in order to help with these situations.

Non-Quality–Related Cultural Dimensions

It's time for another thought experiment.

Think of your current company. You are going to re-found it to make it into the most effective organization in history at doing whatever it is your customer wants it to do. You'll do this by systematically answering a series of important questions, as shown in the table below:

What does your company exist to do?	
List 3–5 skills required in order to be the best in the world at doing this.	
If one team were able to be the best in the world at all of these skills, list 3–8 adjectives you would use to describe one or more of its members.	
Make these adjectives into nouns. These are the core dimensions of the culture your company needs.	

FIGURE 10. Cultural dimensions development grid

Below is a real-world example to illustrate the points above:

What does your company exist to do?	To take wood waste streams and transform them into profitable consumer products.
List 3–5 skills required in order to be the best in the world at doing this.	1. Develop new products from wood waste stream components. 2. Procure reliable sources of wood waste. 3. Efficiently manufacture consumer products from wood waste. 4. Consistently fulfill customer demand for these products. 5. Continually innovate to improve service and profits.
If one team were able to be the best in the world at all of these skills, list 3–8 adjectives you would use to describe one or more of its members.	1. Innovative 2. Productive 3. Collaborative 4. Customer-focused 5. Humble 6. Relentless 7. Data-driven
Make these adjectives into nouns. These are the core dimensions of the culture your company needs.	1. Innovation 2. Productivity 3. Collaboration 4. Customer Focus 5. Humility 6. Relentlessness 7. Data Focus

FIGURE 11. Cultural dimensions development grid example

This method can be used to apply the principles of "Culture Is Everything" more broadly and in non-process-improvement contexts. For process improvement applications, however, we can simply take the six dimensions (Figure 7) as defined and order off the archetypes menu presented in Chapter 3.

One company that I worked for came to a crossroads during my tenure there. Margins were under attack and rapidly diminishing while a combination of new entrants to the market and competitors' vertical integration made it harder each year to hold on to even less profitable customers. Moreover, the customers' expectations regarding service levels increased steadily year-over-year. This company, well over a century old, needed a new company culture in order to survive, as the behaviors which had previously nurtured it had grown toxic over time. But which one?

The pressing need to eliminate waste and improve fulfillment pointed toward a Lean culture. Unfortunately, the company's culture was not well aligned with a Lean culture; while each facility was able to run their operations as they wished, the general manager made all the decisions. Moreover, the company culture was change averse, with decisions being made fairly arbitrarily and with little collaboration and a lot of tribal knowledge. In such aristocratic cultures, large-scale transformations are impossible without leadership being completely in lockstep; in this case, leadership was split into various camps.

Several attempts were made to transform the company, including acquiring different lines of business with better margins and different cultures, hiring and firing several CEOs and company officers, centralizing some functions to reduce the power of the general managers, implementing new information systems, and outsourcing noncore functions. The culture has largely remained unchanged, and company performance has suffered.

This situation is all too common today, especially as leadership turns over.

In retrospect, it would have been better to invest time and resources either in making the existing aristocratic culture more functional by choosing one faction or another and purging the rest, or going deep in a culture closer to the end state the company would need to reach to survive the bruising market conditions and winnow out anyone who wasn't a true believer in that culture. The first option has lower short-term but greater long-term risk than the second. Either would have been preferred over the strategic paralysis that ensued.

This example underscores the need for clarity of vision and strategic realism in determining which culture your company needs. Only top leadership can make such decisions, and in so doing must be vigilant in prioritizing personal career interests firmly beneath the health of the company. The "what" must be established before the "who" can even enter consideration, as culture is simply a tool to help the company do what must be done; the best culture is that which allows for what must be done to happen most naturally and without the need for constant vigilance and oppressive audit practices.[21]

Once we have a firm grasp of what our culture needs to be, we need to unflinchingly inquire into what the culture currently is. Unless you are unusually fortunate, we can expect to uncover some significant gaps between the culture in which we operate today and that which will perfectly suit us for what our company must do tomorrow. This is also the point in the text where I feel compelled to warn you, Gentle Reader, that wherever you may have indicted me for excessive bluntness in my arguments and analysis to this point, you will most assuredly have enough evidence to convict me of that particular crime in the pages to come. I can only note in my defense that I am an engineer by training and by experience and throw myself upon the mercy of a more enlightened and sensitive court if that which follows causes any unintentional offense or repulsion due to its seeming harshness; it is simply a matter of the tone some of us employ when diagnosing the problems which we must solve in order to achieve our mutual goal of an environment in which lofty process improvement goals may be more readily achieved. It is not due to any animus on my part toward any of the company cultures described. If we must drive nails and we currently are equipped with handsaws, I hope you can forgive me for taking a rather dim view of the hammering potential of cutting tools. I make no judgments whatsoever about how well the current culture may have performed in regard to past uses.

FIVE

Assessing Your Company's Culture

"You can get a good handle on a company's culture before you even get inside the building. For example, when companies say, 'We value our employees' but have reserved parking spots, a private cafeteria, and over-the-top offices for the executives, that tells you more than any PR spin."

—STEVE BLANK[22]

Mr. Blank's quote above exposes essential truths in the assessment of company cultures: the culture as communicated can be quite different from the culture as lived; there are objective ways to evaluate culture; and the culture as lived is the most important aspect of any company's culture.

Let's not take Mr. Blank at face value here, though.

Many companies today claim to be customer focused, trumpeting their devotion to customers, their belief that the customer is always right, and the like. Think for a moment of a company which makes such claims.

Does the company you're thinking of engage in the following practices:

- Using phone trees, or otherwise making it difficult to talk to a human being when you have a problem;
- Requiring receipts or proofs of purchase before they will believe you are a customer;
- Not crediting your return until they have taken physical possession of the product you've sent back;
- Refusing to admit to errors on their part;
- Not accepting your favored credit card;
- Having very short return windows;
- Charging restocking fees;
- Charging return postage;

- Understaffing its checkout lines;
- Forcing you as the customer to perform work that used to be done by employees (e.g., scanning your own groceries, ordering from a kiosk, etc.);
- Not always addressing you respectfully in communications;
- Making you wait an inordinate amount of time to be heard;
- Making it difficult for you to escalate your complaint when the first customer-facing employee is lacking?

These sadly common behaviors are not concordant with a culture where the customer comes first. The culture as lived does not match up with the culture as communicated. Each of these behaviors can be objectively assessed (they exist or do not exist, are observed or are not observed), as can the company's response when they are brought to management's attention. When we see such a disconnect between the culture as lived and the culture as communicated, moreover, we tend to have a more negative perception of the company than if it had never communicated such a customer-first value at all: A promise has been broken.

Having confirmed the essential soundness of Mr. Blank's insight, we now must apply it to the development of a cultural assessment tool that demonstrates the virtues of simplicity, objectivity, and comprehensiveness. This will ensure our tool has the flexibility and utility necessary to be worth the practitioner's time.

A hypothetical example would be helpful.

Zappos is an e-commerce shoe business widely regarded as having an attractive company culture. The 10 core values of Zappos are reprinted in their entirety below:[23]

- Deliver WOW Through Service
- Embrace and Drive Change
- Create Fun and a Little Weirdness
- Be Adventurous, Creative, and Open-Minded
- Pursue Growth and Learning
- Build Open and Honest Relationships with Communication
- Build a Positive Team and Family Spirit
- Do More with Less
- Be Passionate and Determined
- Be Humble

Core Value	Decision-Makers	Decisive Information	Decision Authority	Pace of Change	Magnitude of Change	Driver of Change
Deliver WOW Through Service			X			X
Embrace and Drive Change			X	X	X	X
Create Fun and a Little Weirdness			X	X	X	X
Be Adventurous, Creative, and Open-Minded	X		X	X	X	X
Pursue Growth and Learning			X	X	X	X
Build Open and Honest Relationships with Communication						
Build a Positive Team and Family Spirit	X					
Do More with Less		X		X	X	X
Be Passionate and Determined			X			
Be Humble	X					

FIGURE 12. Core Values Translation Matrix

We first must do a bit of translation, as the words chosen by companies to define their cultures tend to vary, and since the culture as a whole may not be the ideal for what the company is seeking to do. For the sake of this example, let's assume Zappos wants to be known for the world-class quality of their products. Let's create a quick matrix showing the relationship between our six dimensions from Figure 7 and these core values:

The Xs in the table above indicate that there may be some relationship between the cultural core value in the row and the cultural dimensions in the columns. This relationship could be positive or negative, large or small. We now must make these relationships more explicit.

The Core Value Translation Matrix allows us to focus the initial discussion with company leadership. For each X, we formulate a question or questions representing that intersection, with the column as the "what" or "who" and the core value as the "how." A questionnaire generated from the above may look like:

1. Who decides whether to proceed with an initiative which promises to WOW through service?
2. Who must approve implementation of a change?
3. Who determines what acceptable "fun" and "weirdness" are?
4. What decisions is a floor employee empowered to make?
5. Who approves an employee's desire to pursue a learning or growth opportunity?
6. How creative may employees get before needing to seek management approval?
7. Who defines what a positive team and family spirit entails?
8. Why do you need to exhort employees to be humble?
9. How often do basic job processes change?
10. How often do employees engage in growth and learning opportunities?
11. How often do employees drive productivity initiatives?
12. How big of a change can employees make on their own authority?
13. Who determines what changes will be implemented?
14. What evidence is required for "doing more with less"?
15. What information is required to support implementing a change?
16. What kinds of information are important to impart for there to be "open and honest relationships with communication"?

Where there are gaps in the alignment, we should ask additional questions to fill in information regarding how the company views these areas.[24] For example, if nothing in the company's core values indicates a preference for data- or gut-driven decision-making, asking questions such as: "When there is a conflict between available but incomplete data and a key leader's gut instinct, which do you embrace?" would be in order.

The answers to these questions form a view of the company's culture as leadership sees it, a starting framework for assessing this culture as communicated, understood, and lived.[25] We may now apply objective scales to each dimension as we quantify and further define the type of company culture leadership is describing.

For each cultural dimension shown in the tables below, we can score the company's answers to the above questions.

Leveraging these scales along with our prework questionnaire results, we can now create our cultural assessment tool. Following our Communicated, Understood, and Lived lenses for culture, we will ask slightly different questions to different audiences in order to provide a full picture of how the company's culture is functioning relative to the six dimensions most important to process improvement strategies. While I provide a typical questionnaire in Figure 19, the practitioner

Rating	Criteria
5	Employees at the lowest level of organizational hierarchy are fully empowered to stop production, satisfy customers, employ company resources, and manage risk at their discretion.
4	Supervisors and above are fully empowered to stop production, satisfy customers, employ company resources, and manage risk at their discretion.
3	Managers and above are fully empowered to stop production, satisfy customers, employ company resources, and manage risk at their discretion.
2	Junior executives are fully empowered to stop production, satisfy customers, employ company resources, and manage risk at their discretion.
1	Senior executives are fully empowered to stop production, satisfy customers, employ company resources, and manage risk at their discretion.

FIGURE 13. Decision-Makers (DM) Dimension Objective Scale

Rating	Criteria
5	Where data contradicts experience, data always wins.
4	Where data contradicts experience, data usually wins.
3	Decisions are made by balancing data and experience.
2	Where experience contradicts data, experience usually wins.
1	Where experience contradicts data, experience always wins.

FIGURE 14. Decisive Information (DI) Dimension Objective Scale

Rating	Criteria
5	Where decisions are in contradiction between two decision-makers, the more credible decision-maker always wins.
4	Where decisions are in contradiction between two decision-makers, the more credible decision-maker usually wins.
3	Decisions are made by balancing organizational rank and credibility.
2	Where decisions are in contradiction between two decision-makers, the higher-ranking decision-maker usually wins.
1	Where decisions are in contradiction between two decision-makers, the higher-ranking decision-maker always wins.

FIGURE 15. Decision Authority (DA) Dimension Objective Scale

Rating	Criteria
5	Employees expect core job functions to change more frequently than once per month.
4	Employees expect core job functions to change approximately once per month.
3	Employees expect core job functions to change approximately once per quarter.
2	Employees expect core job functions to change approximately once per year.
1	Employees expect core job functions to change less frequently than once per year.

FIGURE 16. Pace of Change (CP) Dimension Objective Scale

Rating	Criteria
5	The majority of employees embrace major changes in the company's products, services, policies, processes, and strategies.
4	The majority of employees embrace minor changes in the company's products, services, policies, processes, and strategies.
3	The majority of employees neither resist nor embrace major changes in the company's products, services, policies, processes, and strategies.
2	The majority of employees resist major changes in the company's products, services, policies, processes, and strategies.
1	The majority of employees resist minor changes in the company's products, services, policies, processes, and strategies.

FIGURE 17. Magnitude of Change (CM) Dimension Objective Scale

Rating	Criteria
5	Change originates with the employees performing the work.
4	Change originates with middle management.
3	Change originates with the company's top leadership.
2	Change originates with external consultants.
1	Change originates with market, regulatory, supply-chain, or customer pressures.

FIGURE 18. Driver of Change (CD) Dimension Objective Scale

will want to tailor this instrument as needed to best represent the company being assessed. We use a 5-point Likert scale to assist in the aggregation and quantification of the results.

Due to the nature of the objective scales, it is not strictly necessary to have multiple questions per dimension. We do so above so as to provide an internal check on the results and ensure the statements are clear to respondents. The statements in Figure 19 speak to the culture as lived. The next series of questions will help us assess the culture as understood by the employees, which of course may yield different results.

#	Statement	Strongly Disagree	Disagree	Neither Agree nor Disagree	Agree	Strongly Agree
1	I am fully empowered to stop production, satisfy customers, employ company resources, and manage risk at my discretion.					
2	If a situation comes up where data doesn't agree with a key leader's experience or opinion, the final decision will be made based upon the data, not the leader's experience or opinion.					
3	If two leaders disagree, the higher-ranking leader will make the final decision.					
4	I expect the major functions of my job to change in less than a month.					
5	When major changes to my company's products, services, policies, processes, or strategies are announced, the majority of our employees will actively support the proposed changes.					
6	Most changes in this company originate with the employee(s) who perform the work impacted by the change.					
7	The final decision to stop production, satisfy customers, employ company resources, or manage risk must be made by a senior executive.					
8	If a situation comes up where data doesn't agree with a key leader's experience or opinion, the final decision will be made based upon the leader's experience or opinion, not the data.					
9	If two leaders disagree, the more credible and knowledgeable leader will make the final decision.					
10	I do not expect the major functions of my job to change this year.					
11	When minor changes to my company's products, services, policies, processes, or strategies are announced, the majority of our employees will actively resist the proposed changes.					
12	Most changes in this company originate because the government, customers, or our supply-chain partners require them to be made.					

FIGURE 19. Sample Assessment Tool—Lived Section

#	Statement	SD	D	N	A	SA
13	My company believes I should be fully empowered to stop production, satisfy customers, employ company resources, and manage risk at my discretion.					
14	If a situation comes up where data doesn't agree with a key leader's experience or opinion, my company believes the final decision should be made based upon the data, not the leader's experience or opinion.					
15	If two leaders disagree, my company believes the higher-ranking leader should make the final decision.					
16	My company believes I should expect the major functions of my job to change in less than a month.					
17	When major changes to my company's products, services, policies, processes, or strategies are announced, my company believes the majority of our employees will actively support the proposed changes.					
18	My company believes that most changes in this company should originate with the employee(s) who perform the work impacted by the change.					
19	My company believes that the final decision to stop production, satisfy customers, employ company resources, or manage risk must be made by a senior executive.					
20	If a situation comes up where data doesn't agree with a key leader's experience or opinion, my company believes that the final decision will be made based upon the leader's experience or opinion, not the data.					
21	If two leaders disagree, my company believes that the more credible and knowledgeable leader should make the final decision.					
22	My company believes I should not expect the major functions of my job to change this year.					
23	When minor changes to my company's products, services, policies, processes, or strategies are announced, my company believes that the majority of our employees will actively resist the proposed changes.					
24	My company believes that most changes in this company should originate because the government, customers, or our supply-chain partners require them to be made.					

FIGURE 20. Sample Assessment Tool—Understood Section

With Understood and Lived covered, we have several options for dealing with how the culture has been Communicated:

1. Grade the prework questionnaire from leadership directly using the objective scales and review with leadership;
2. Give leadership a separate questionnaire with slight variations of the Understood questionnaire;
3. Where communications materials exist, use the prework questionnaire responses in conjunction with these communication materials to apply the objective scales and determine a score.

Whichever method is used, and applying the mean result for the employee questionnaires for each dimension, we can populate the summary scoring table in an example below:

Dimension	Desired	Communicated	Understood	Lived
Decision-Makers (DM)	5	5	3.45	3.05
Decisive Information (DI)	3	2	1.90	1.50
Decision Authority (DA)	1	1	1.35	2.40
Pace of Change (CP)	5	4	3.25	2.75
Magnitude of Change (CM)	5	5	4.50	3.12
Driver of Change (CD)	1	1	2.16	3.05

FIGURE 21. Culture Assessment Validation Scorecard Example

Figure 21 demonstrates precision to two decimal places and relies upon mean responses; my more analytical brethren can and should take exception to such quantification methods and are free to deviate from the example as they deem useful. The point is simply to provide some gauge for the distance between these categories, not to offer a defense of any given number. The bigger the gap, the more work we'll have to do in order to close it. Moreover, this tends to be a moving target over time, especially for smaller organizations where turnover may drive some swings in the result. For the most part, though, behaviors stemming from workplace cultures tend to be fairly resistant to large-scale changes. If you suspect your culture is more fluid than the norm, you'd be well advised to take the temperature of the baseline assessment several times and perhaps stratify within organizational structure much as you would do with any survey instrument. The caution against prizing what people say over what they actually do still holds.

In the next chapter, we'll tease out the implications of differences in culture between that Desired, Communicated, Understood, and Lived—and how these differences inform the development of a strategy to close these gaps and more fully align the culture as Lived with that Desired.

SIX

Desired, Communicated, Understood, and Lived Cultures

"Improving quality requires a culture change, not just a new diet."

—PHIL CROSBY[26]

In Chapter 2, we introduced the distinction between company culture as communicated, as understood, and as lived. In Chapter 4, we added another distinction: culture as desired (or needed). It is now time to discuss the relevance of these distinctions in our efforts to drive successful process improvement in our companies.

Phil Crosby, whom we quote above, is one of the most important thinkers and practitioners in the quality movement.[27] Like W. Edwards Deming before him, he realized that sustained continuous improvement required not just new tools but a new way of thinking about business. It was not feasible in the hierarchical, management-by-fear corporate culture of the time to simply start producing higher-quality products and services; it went particularly against the grain of change avoidance and strict accountability for perceived failure.

Let's put ourselves in the shoes of a young Crosby or Deming, occupying a lower management rung in a company epitomizing our Aristocratic archetype. We know that we need to improve our quality and customer service to thrive, but the don't-rock-the-boat grain of the company and the sheer distance between us and the real decision-makers in the wedding-cake corporate structure is daunting. The Six Sigma archetype of an orderly, data-driven company constantly getting a little better every day is where we want and need to go, but how do we get there?

Setting aside the leadership engagement and change management aspects of this challenge for the moment (we'll return to these later), we begin by getting our arms firmly around the culture we desire: Six Sigma. Our Validation Scorecard approach can help:

Dimension	Desired	Communicated	Understood	Lived
Decision-Makers (DM)	3	3	3	3
Decisive Information (DI)	5	5	5	5
Decision Authority (DA)	3	3	3	3
Pace of Change (CP)	2	2	2	2
Magnitude of Change (CM)	2	2	2	2
Driver of Change (CD)	3	3	3	3

FIGURE 22. Culture Validation Scorecard Example

Applying the objective scales for each of our six dimensions in Chapter 5 and referring to the archetype definition in Chapter 3 and tweaking just a hair for the scenario provided, we come up with the desired cultural scores for each dimension seen above. The major changes we're looking for relative to the Aristocratic culture we have comes down to accepting a bit more change than we're wired for and having management drive that change. The company is already well wired for making decisions based on data, at least in the sense that data doesn't alienate key decision-makers or imply the need for sweeping changes.

For this effort to be a tremendous success, we want the difference between the culture as desired, communicated, understood, and lived to be 0 (zero). We want to hit the target that we're aiming toward here.

Following through with our scenario, we've convinced top leadership and middle management to agree with our plan to improve quality. They see the value in the new culture and will actively work to help transform the culture. That desired culture column represents perfectly our shared vision for the future of our company.

Even in an Aristocratic culture, we can't simply issue a memo and expect everyone to fall in line. There is considerable organizational inertia that must be overcome first. Our employees need to fully understand our desired culture, why we're moving in that direction, and how their behavior will need to change along the way. We must clearly, consistently, and constantly communicate this information to them if we are to avoid gaps in culture As Communicated and As Understood.

Further, we need to build their confidence and skills during the transition and thereby create the habits we will require them to maintain once the transition is complete. We want them to embrace smaller changes needed to improve quality and to be willing to experiment to find better ways of doing things, but before that, we must ensure that past practices which made our employees so risk averse are done away with. If bureaucratic barriers were erected to make minor changes more difficult, they must be torn down. If employees who advocated for change were punished for nonconformity, they must now be celebrated as heroes of our new culture.

It may be helpful to think of these transitional changes geared toward closing the gap between culture *as desired* with culture a*s lived* as building bridges, as seen in the illustration below:

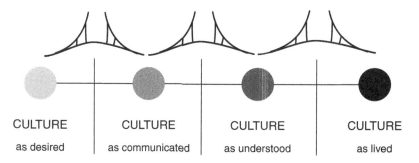

FIGURE 23. Bridging gaps between culture as desired and as lived

The better bridges we build, the closer we come to living our new culture completely. We shall now take a look at specific chasms to be spanned in our quest to make the culture we desire that which we live.

From Desired to Communicated

Before we can effectively communicate the culture we desire, we must first ensure that we fully understand the culture we want and then focus on articulating this vision as clearly as possible for a wide variety of audiences. We have previously leveraged archetypes and defined a spectrum of behaviors that we quantified in order to establish a target and ensure our chosen culture will be capable of helping our company do what it must do. This is necessary and important work, but not sufficient for the purpose of effective communication to all organizational levels. To bridge the gap between our desired culture and the cultural norms we communicate, we need to reach for the right tool: we need a *meme*.

You've probably heard of memes; they are the common currency of the Information Age. A meme is "a cultural item that is transmitted by repetition and replication in a manner analogous to the biological transmission of genes."[28] It is the manner by which cultural norms proliferate. The trick is to pursue this transmission purposefully, through careful husbandry of the culture, rather than by simply sowing the wind with the seeds of culture.

Made to Stick by Chip and Dan Heath is the Farmer's Almanac for the meme generation.[29] In this book, which I heartily recommend, the authors introduce a blueprint for creating highly memorable memes defined by the acronym SUCCES (my definition and examples are provided below for the acronym's elements; any errors in interpretation are therefore my own):

- **Simple.** Strip the idea down to its very essence. In the context of company culture, precision in the definition of what we are trying to do as an organization points the way. American general Colin Powell's mission statement prior to the 1991 Gulf War was a marvel of simplicity: "Forcibly eject the Iraqi Republican Guard from the Kuwaiti Theater of Operations." Everyone from private to four-star general could understand the war aim and apply it successfully no matter what their role was in the conflict.
- **Unexpectedness.** That which surprises us lodges in our memory. Counterintuitive insight wins here. Apple's "Think Different" advertising campaign is a memorable example: It's built around an ungrammatical phrase that rings false

upon the ears yet underscores the need to abandon stuffy old ways of thinking. Former British prime minister Winston Churchill famously responded to a grammar scold bemoaning dangling prepositions by saying, "That is something up with which I shall not put."

- **Concreteness.** We spend a lot of time in the world of the abstract while crafting strategies and designing cultures. Big, lofty words are the norm, usually at the expense of crisp thinking in plain English that anyone can grasp. Wiggle room increases gaps between the living and desired cultures—gaps we need to eliminate. When at the end of his novel *1984* George Orwell sought to indelibly define the dystopian future he warned humanity against, he did so in the most concrete terms possible: "If you want a vision of the future, imagine a boot stamping on a human face—forever." That is far more evocative and memorable than condemning corruption, political violence, deceit, totalitarianism, socialism, thuggery, slavery, or any of the host of evils he details earlier in the book. It is absolutely chilling—and very concrete.

- **Credibility.** Use details and invoke authorities to provide a reason for your audience to believe in your idea. When outsider Carly Fiorina took over the reins at Hewlett Packard, she linked herself to the company's founding myth by constantly referring to the garage in which the founders built the first products the company made. She sought to return the company to that spirit of innovation—and to make it clear that she was openly assuming the mantle of these legendary business leaders. Whatever one makes of her tenure, it is clear that HP employees understood what she was trying to do.

- **Emotional.** If you want us to do something, make us feel something. Apathy is the friend of inertia. My favorite example of this came from General George Washington's defusing of the Newburgh Conspiracy near the end of the Revolutionary War. The Continental Congress had failed to pay its soldiers, leading disgruntled officers to gather in New York and foment an uprising against it. Washington, ever blessed with excellent intelligence, learned of the meeting and called his own assembly of these officers. After first condemning the unseemliness of the actions they were considering and imploring them to place their faith in their general and their government, Washington withdrew from his pocket a letter from a member of Congress and endeavored to read it to them, but found he could not and paused, reaching for his glasses: "Gentlemen, you must pardon me. I have grown old in the service of my country and now find that I am growing blind." Tears streamed down the officers' cheeks as they voted unanimously their faith in Congress and country, a vote carried by the affection wrought in their hearts for the public frailty of their mighty commander.[30] We think with our brains but act with our hearts.

- **Stories.** As you might discern from the examples above and throughout this book, this is the indispensable principle to me. Humans are storytelling creatures; this is what distinguishes us most clearly from the rest of the animal kingdom. We use stories to make sense of the world from when we first begin to comprehend language straight through to our final breaths. We hunger for stories: myths, mysteries—and memes, which are nothing more than the shortest of short stories. W. Edward Deming's famous Red Bead Experiment—a story told and retold by quality professionals for over a century now—wasn't really an experiment at all. It was a story. It had a beginning, a middle, and an end as well as a villain (uncaring management blaming workers who didn't control the process for its negative outcomes). Six Sigma devotees tell stories about how even processes that perform well 99.9% of the time yield horrific results that we must find completely unacceptable when dragged into the spotlight. Genichi Taguchi did much the same when describing the terrible cost of variation in processes even when they ostensibly perform to specification. Lean thinkers know full well how important it is to tell cautionary tales of the hell wrought by overproduction, the path to which is paved with the noble intention of "staying busy." Stories survive long after the books in which they were written have crumbled to dust. Just ask Homer.

Return with me to our example from earlier in the chapter: We want to move toward a Six Sigma culture from the stereotypical Aristocratic culture we have today. Unfortunately, not everyone in the company understands what Six Sigma is, much less what a Six Sigma culture might be. We need some way of effectively transmitting the values of our new culture. After reviewing the SUCCES model above, we developed the following meme:

Engineered to Perfection

"This is a stone block.

"It is a very large block, weighing about 2.5 tons, a little bit lighter than a compact car. Its big brothers—called casing stones—were 5 feet long, 5 feet high, and 6 feet deep, weighing about 15 tons. These casing stones were found at one site to have been placed with accuracy to within 5 thousandths of an inch, a gap of 2 hundredths of an inch having been left for the mortar that filled the space between blocks.

"These 2.3 million blocks were brought together in a square base, then built up with sloping sides until the structure converged 455 feet up. Each face of the completed structure aimed in the cardinal directions—north, south, east, and west—with a deviation of just 0.015 percent, which is 99.985% accuracy. The sides differed in length by no more than 8 inches, or 99.912% accuracy.[31]

"This sort of precision takes a lot of work. No building built on Earth today requires this level of precision—it takes too long to build and costs too much money. The engineering and construction processes involved in such an undertaking are immense. It's considered not worth it to take that level of care in your work today.

"The engineers and builders of the structure just described are long gone. They've been dead for over 4,500 years, in fact.

"The building in question is the Great Pyramid of Khufu at Giza, the earliest and last of the Seven Great Wonders of the World in existence today. The Pharaoh Khufu is remembered today because of the care taken by the ancient Egyptians in building the very best. We will be remembered in the future, provided we follow their example.

"Each of you is being given a much smaller, lighter block than Khufu used. On it you'll see we've written 'Engineered to Perfection' to remind you of what we're building at this company. By bringing these blocks together and making tiny changes in how we do things each day, we'll build our own great wonder: a company that will last as long as the Great Pyramid has. Your grandchildren and their grandchildren will know what you have built here.

"The mortar we'll be using is something called Six Sigma."

Well, we've certainly told a story. There was a surprising revelation. It is simple—precision helps us build to last. Credibility was assured by referencing the longest-lasting and impressive large construction on the planet. What could be more concrete than stone? There's the emotional tie-in: lasting greatness. Perhaps it could have more directly referenced Six Sigma, although of course it may be sufficient for most in the company to just understand that that methodology is helping them build a great organization.

From Communicated to Understood

If we believe that memes are the most important vector of communication and that the Heaths' SUCCES method helps us to craft highly effective memes, we still may run into issues with the interpretation of the meme. This leads to yawning gaps between what we have communicated about culture and what our personnel actually understand it to mean.

A variety of factors may lead to noise in the communication:

- **Cultural differences.** Large organizations sometimes span the world, and this can lead to very different meanings of symbols or words used in memes. When I was a cadet at the United States Air Force Academy, freshmen cadets were required to loudly greet any upperclassmen they passed on campus while running back and forth to their next duty. There were many times when having someone yell "Good afternoon, sir!" was not desired, whereupon the upperclassman would hold up his index and middle fingers in a hand sign called "post" that meant "Be quiet." One afternoon, I noticed a couple of British exchange officers laughing uncontrollably as they watched upperclassmen use this hand sign on a long line of freshmen running to formation. It turns out that the sign Winston Churchill used to indicate "V for Victory" has an additional, vulgar meaning in the United Kingdom. They thought that the upperclassmen were insulting every freshman who ran by and found it hysterically funny.

- **Generational differences.** Senior leadership in any company is quite often significantly older than the most junior members, which can lead to misunderstandings. I recall one such senior leader getting blank stares when he relayed a favorite anecdote that turned upon breaking off a relationship because his paramour had too many nines in her phone number. The leader had grown up with rotary telephones; dialing nines on these often caused physical discomfort. Absent this shared experience, the anecdote made no sense to the audience.

- **Gender differences.** Men and women often have different speaking styles. In the opening of the movie *Patton* (1970), U.S. Army general George S. Patton, Jr. delivers a dramatic speech to his assembled soldiers on the eve of a great battle. His oration is florid with profanity (he was no doubt seeking to be concrete with his memes), a characteristic that his men seemed to relish. The reaction would no doubt have been very different had he been addressing a gathering of the Daughters of the American Revolution. Contrast this with Eva Peron's final speech to the Argentinian people, where she denies her own political ambitions while praising her husband (the dictator Juan Peron) and basks in the love of her people. Patton's emotional impact is visceral—that of the stern father requiring the utmost of his boys. Peron appeals to the bond between children and their mother.

- **Educational differences.** Organizations often vary widely in terms of formal education. The use of academic jargon, flowery language, or complicated arguments may decrease comprehension. Plain, clear speech and writing will go a long way to ensure your audience gets your message. Save the poetry for writing books about culture and process improvement, when you can fully rely on your audience to be comprised of geniuses of the first order. (Sucking up surely can't hurt.)

- **Short attention spans.** We consume vast quantities of information over the course of our day, and—Look! That dog's wearing a sweater!

- **WIIFM issues.** "What's in it for me?" is shorthand for lack of relevance in content. Senior leadership likes to talk at the strategic level—that's what they spend most of their time at work doing. Frontline personnel have more pressing and tactical concerns. If you can connect the dots to their daily lives, the message will be better understood.

As helpful as the recommendations above are, the best one was offered by physicist Richard Feynman: "If you can't explain something to a first-year student, then you haven't really understood." When crafting your communication to all levels of the organization, aim squarely at the most junior employee. Then ensure you have some way of testing how well the message has been understood, preferably in a manner that requires the active engagement of the audience.

We had just formed a brand-new quality improvement team to help support a company's transformation to a Six Sigma culture. Knowing that it would be important to be able to explain what we were trying to do with applied statistics in terms everyone could understand, my manager had us all develop and rehearse 30-second "elevator speeches" to get across the value we were delivering. These were called "elevator speeches" because they were intended to simulate a chance meeting with a senior leadership member in the company in an elevator where the question, "So, what are you working on?" might come up.

Now, I don't know that any of us actually wound up taking that elevator ride. But we all emerged from that exercise with a much better understanding of what we were doing and why. Asking your teams to articulate what precisely they would do differently after hearing the culture communication can help ensure they truly understood the message. Having them recast it in their own terms may be even more useful, as that personal ownership is a very powerful motivator.

From Understood to Lived

We humans are creatures of habit. We tend to repeat the same patterns of behavior again and again, even when these patterns are clearly counterproductive. Fundamental change is extremely difficult if not outright impossible for us, despite our best intentions to follow through with these changes. How many of us have vowed to lose weight, work out regularly, learn a new language, spend more time with our children, or finally finish reading an amazing book on culture and process improvement only to drift away from our goals? How many of us have read *The 7 Habits of Highly Effective People* by Stephen Covey and vowed solemnly to adopt each and every one only to find ourselves a short time later struggling to get through the day the way we always had? Eli Goldratt, author of *The Goal* and father of the Theory of Constraints, used to torture himself by asking fans of his book what they were doing to apply his principles. The answers were almost invariably a great disappointment.

By contrast, bad habits spread like wildfire. Let one of your kids have ice cream for dinner and watch how fast that becomes a family tradition. I used to run the engineering function for a large warehouse distribution company and was responsible for developing and deploying their labor standards to help improve productivity. We spent months figuring out ways to get more employee time into tracked functions so that they could be plugged into the bonus system and align incentives with work. We at last reached the summit and had one final challenge to conquer: how to ensure that employees couldn't simply put in the wrong code in their handheld devices and bypass supervisor approval in the process. At last we had it—we would create small cards with bar codes on them that the supervisors would have, which would require the worker to get preapproval for things like breaks or training time and thereby prevent abuse.

It took our teammates all of 18 hours at one site to figure out that they could scan a code, back the cursor up, and put in the code they wanted from memory. In 72 hours that "best practice" was being faithfully followed throughout the company. I ran the reports from the labor management system and could see the culture metastasize in near real time.

It was a deeply humbling experience.

Mind you, all of this took place after months of strategy meetings, collaboration with the field, a very well-designed communication plan, and an enormous burning platform in the form of ongoing layoffs, cratering stock price, eroding margins, and lost business. Yet when push came to shove, the culture fought back—and won.

I relay this tale of woe, not because I know it will amuse you to know that someone with the audacity to write about company culture has failed miserably to change it in the past, but rather to highlight just how difficult it is to bridge the gap from culture as understood to culture as lived. Believe me, those teammates who devised the ingenious workaround understood what we were trying to do and why. The change was not all that inconvenient; indeed, they had already partially undermined the whole process by simply making duplicates of the bar code cards so they didn't have to go to the supervisor at all (the supervisor still needed to approve it in the system on the back end, but they could technically pencil-whip that).

At root the problem was simply that our teammates resented being measured. Not all of them, surely—the ones who were generally at the top of the bonus payouts seemed to like that aspect of the job. But from what I gathered from the various meetings during which I was brought in to explain and defend the labor management system, a majority of the teammates simply felt that that sort of measurement led to manifestly unfair, unsafe, and often insulting work practices. It ran against the grain of the company culture as they understood it.

If we want our employees to live the new culture—to truly embrace it—that kind of friction simply cannot stand. Inertia will overcome all of our best efforts to change.

I often relay an anecdote concerning chimps in a cage from an experiment some decades ago in order to explain this phenomenon. There were five chimpanzees placed in a large metal cage. A bunch of bananas was suspended from the top of the cage over a metal ladder.

Chimps love bananas.

The first chimp climbed up the ladder and grabbed a banana—whereupon a cruel scientist promptly sprayed him with a jet of water from a fire hose.

Chimps hate being wet.

They remove one chimp from the cage and introduce a new one. He promptly tries to climb the ladder—whereupon his fellow chimps beat him silly. Chimps hate being wet.

This goes on with one chimp being removed and a new one introduced until no chimp that had witnessed the fire hose being used remained in the cage. Still, whenever a new chimp would head toward the ladder, the other chimps would beat him up.

How come?

"Because that's just the way we do things around here."

If we're really going to break such deeply engrained behaviors and replace them with ones more amenable to the desired culture, we have to understand why that fire hose was needed.

Chimps love bananas. They will go to considerable lengths to obtain them. In order to break them of a behavior—getting bananas and eating them—which they have found to be very beneficial in the past, we must employ either a bigger reward or a bigger punishment for them. Chimps hate being wet more than they love bananas.

Despite our pretensions, we humans still act a lot like chimps. We are motivated by incentives and punishments in much the way they are. That can be used to our advantage in bridging the gap between culture as desired and culture as lived.

Let's talk incentives first, since we hope these will be sufficient and punishments won't be necessary.

In my story about the ingenious warehouse workers above, I mentioned a bonus system. If their productivity as measured in lines per hour were high enough, every quarter they would receive a bonus check. This would be funded in large part through the reduction in overtime from the increased productivity. The problem we ran into was that overtime paid one-and-a-half times their regular hourly wage and the bonus offered only a small fraction of this amount—they would lose money on this proposition while working harder. Then incentives were actually heading in the wrong direction.

How about the punishment?

In that case, we were already struggling to find and retain solid workers. Many of our sites were located near other distribution operations. In the race for talent, these competitors would often increase wages and lure our best teammates away in the process. Moreover, it could take a long time to find and hire a replacement—which would lead to higher overtime rates for everyone else to cover. This led to a situation where supervisors were extremely reluctant to write up or terminate anyone for almost any reason. When this fact became apparent, it spread as quickly as the news about the handheld device hack did.

This is not to criticize these employees. They worked hard, looked out for the customer, and were to a very large extent great people to work with. They were responding rationally to the situation the company placed them in.

I wonder what would have happened if we had taken the plunge and really made the incentives worthwhile. The company gave away a car in each region every year, a very popular program that required perfect attendance in order to qualify for the lottery. A sizable number of teammates strove for that perfect attendance as a result, which really helped. Perhaps we could have done something similar with a bonus of several thousand dollars in play—something that would really help our teammates out.

As a lifelong operations person, I also know that when it comes to culture change, you will often need to make an example of someone. Thankfully, it usually takes only one. If there is someone in the organization who has sizable influence and no intention of living the culture you desire, get them out. Fast. And make it very clear that the reason you're doing so is that they have chosen not to embrace the new culture. If they happen to be fairly senior in the company, you get the added benefit of having a desirable slot in which to place someone who is on board with the new culture. Addition by subtraction. As they move up, you gain another position to fill with a cultural hero. Before you know it, "the way we do things around here" will closely resemble the desired culture.

I was having this discussion with a terrific supply-chain software company recently. I put the question to the CEO and founder as to how you make sure that the culture is lived, and his response fascinated me. To paraphrase: "I know we're living it because one of my people came to me recently to inform me they were letting someone go who had failed to live up to our culture. They were informing me—not asking my permission. They knew this person needed to go because everyone is expected to live our culture."

Chinese Communist leader Mao Zedong literally wrote the book on guerilla warfare following his successful campaign to drive the Nationalists out of mainland China. In it, he describes a three-phased process, which, with a little modification and much less gunfire, can guide any sizable change effort:

1. **Establish revolutionary cadres.** These are the true believers, the diehard proponents of change which form the nucleus of the new organization.
2. **Undermine the status quo.** The old order must be relentlessly attacked. Our combination of reward and punishment can help considerably here. Most of the time and effort involved occur within this phase.
3. **When you're strong enough, take on and defeat the forces of the status quo.** This doesn't mean you need a majority of the team to be true believers—Malcolm Gladwell, in his seminal work *The Tipping Point*, suggests you need about one-third of the organization to do this.[32]

I must also point out at this point that where I have employed historical or political examples, I do so not to endorse any party, faction, governmental system, or movement. I am illustrating the underlying principles with examples that I hope readers can relate to while passing no judgment whatsoever as to whether or not the characters in these stories are good or bad people with the best or worst of intentions. For the record, I take a dim view of soaking monkeys, even when doing so yields interesting social science data.

Now that we've digested this disparate collection of wisdom, we can distill it down to the following helpful tips for bridging the gap between culture as understood and as lived:

- Understand the attachment that teammates have to the current cultural norms: What do they like about it? What do they dislike?
- Identify the influencers within the organization and seek their help in transitioning to the desired culture. We will provide useful tips for doing this in the chapters to follow.
- Tailor your message to different audiences in a way that emphasizes the benefits of the desired culture to their day-to-day lives. Put yourself in their shoes and ask, "What would most appeal to these folks about our desired culture?"
- Provide meaningful rewards to those engaging in the new cultural behaviors. What we reward we will get more of.
- Act swiftly to remove influential die-hard opponents of the desired culture, if not from the company, then at least from having such influential positions within it. As Abraham Lincoln observed, "A house divided against itself cannot stand."
- Discuss the prior cultural norms and behaviors as artifacts of the company's past, emphasizing the positive aspects of the new culture. "We used to have to ask a supervisor for permission to halt the line so we could address a quality issue. Now, every employee is empowered to push that big red button so we can fix a problem before it gets to our customers."
- Before we can ask our employees to live the desired culture, we must do so ourselves—very publicly. Before we can ask anyone else to believe, we must be true believers ourselves. Beware of those who say one thing while doing another. Hypocrisy is the acid of credibility.

SEVEN

The Fork in the Road

Conform, Reform, or Transform

"Alice came to a fork in the road. 'Which road do I take?' she asked. 'Where do you want to go?' responded the Cheshire Cat. 'I don't know,' Alice answered. 'Then, said the Cat, 'it doesn't matter.'"

—LEWIS CARROLL[33]

We've honed our message, chosen our desired culture, evaluated our current culture, and now we have come to a crossroads. What is the best path forward toward our desired culture?

We can label the roads representing our choices as Conform, Reform, and Transform.

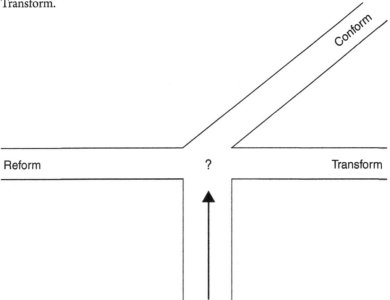

FIGURE 24. The cultural crossroads

- **Conform.** Go with the grain of the current culture insofar as possible wherever the behaviors and values of it are not in direct contradiction to those of the desired culture.
- **Reform.** Make minor changes to the current culture in order to bring it closer to the norms of the desired culture.
- **Transform.** Jettison the old culture and replace it with the desired culture.

In deciding which of these roads to proceed down, we should first recognize that each option has its own trade-offs between risk and level of effort to consider, as shown below:

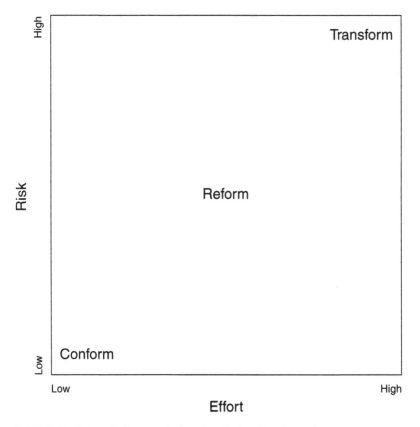

FIGURE 25. Risk and effort matrix for cultural migration alternatives

The Conform strategy works best when faced with a deeply entrenched culture with a less-than-compelling burning platform for change. If employees are very invested in a culture, particularly if it is long-lived or deeply entwined with the company's brand, running across the grain of that culture while attempting to build an environment more conducive to process improvement is going to be very time-consuming and difficult. A good example might be attempting to introduce Lean on a large scale at a company strongly driven by compliance principles. While in theory one can write Lean thinking into "The Book" by which all employees operate, in practice we tend to miss opportunities to reduce waste due to the rigid hierarchies within the company. Merely launching a series of cross-functional kaizen blitzes in such an environment is likely to create drama out of all proportion to the benefit derived due to the anarchic appearance of the effort to a very buttoned-down management team. If some way could be found to move in harmony with the culture, great progress could be made.

A real-world example of this may be found with UPS's focus on driver routes which do not require left turns. UPS is a compliance-driven company, with a strong industrial engineering mentality, seeking to save seconds in order to save millions of dollars at high transaction volumes. Lean may gain a foothold in a company like UPS through its utility as a way to gain small efficiencies, say, by identifying opportunities such as finding ways to route drivers in such a way that they don't lose time waiting for traffic to clear so they can turn left, an application of spaghetti diagramming with time rather than distance as the determining factor. From there it is a short leap to hunt down other time lost due to waiting. When enough credibility has been built, the Lean practitioner could at last begin to tackle the enormous overproduction waste endemic to large distribution operations where "keeping busy" at all times is prized.

The Conform strategy offers several important advantages:

- Ease of effort
- Low risk of failure
- Natural buy-in
- Faster implementation

It also presents several pitfalls:

- Culture may regress back to prior norms
- Change may not be sufficient to accomplish company objectives

- Appetite for change may decrease
- Negative aspects of culture could be ratified by not being changed

Reform is an attractive middle-ground strategy that affords significant change for some increased effort and risk. With a reform strategy, we will shave off the rough edges of our old culture and smooth them out with modified behaviors and norms from our desired culture. This is a viable option when the appetite for change is moderate and the legacy culture is not uniformly firmly entrenched.

A good example of a reform strategy in action occurred at Bank of America in the wake of the mortgage crisis of 2008. The company had previously pursued a strategy of becoming the largest mortgage lender, acquiring Countrywide, the largest mortgage originator in the United States, earlier that year. Bank of America so respected Countrywide's accomplishments in the mortgage business that it largely abandoned its own mortgage practices in favor of Countrywide's.

Once the crisis hit, Bank of America realized that the Countrywide mortgage lending culture was not sustainable in an era of heightened regulatory scrutiny and financial pressures. A major effort was launched to assess every process in the mortgage business for risk and regulatory compliance, develop business controls to mitigate risk and ensure compliance, and build a robust audit and testing regimen to make sure that this new culture took hold.

This application of reform strategy to an organization forged in a merger under intense scrutiny and financial pressure is the textbook example of this concept. While both Bank of America and Countrywide had long-standing cultures in place within their respective mortgage businesses, the acquisition and bringing together of different teams has shaken the status quo up. The financial crisis struck a major blow to the confidence of the combined organization and the uncertainty of the future created a burning platform for change which was undeniable. Full cultural transformation wasn't possible due to time and money considerations and the instability of the regulatory environment of the time.

The advantages of the Reform strategy are:

- Sizable changes in cultural behavior and norms are achievable
- Buy-in can be attained with relatively low effort as long as the need to change is apparent

- Implementation can be fast, with sufficient resources committed to the change management effort

Disadvantages may include:

- Culture may regress once burning platform for change cools down
- Change may not be sufficient to achieve company objectives
- Reform requires expertise in both current and desired cultures, which may be hard to come by

The Transform strategy is often embraced without full consideration of the magnitude of the effort involved. Transformations often come about in times of absolute desperation, when the business environment has so degraded that there may quite literally be nothing left to lose. McKinsey & Company, a renowned consulting firm known for its efforts to help turn around failing companies, estimates that 70% of all cultural transformations fail.[34]

Failures abound due to a host of causes. First, companies which are failing often are hampered with highly dysfunctional cultures, which can be very difficult to fix. Layoffs in the recent past may make leadership reluctant to remove employees who will not make the transition to the new culture. The leadership team, the locus of cultural generation, may well have lost credibility or turned over in the run-up to the transformation effort, making it more difficult to leverage the trust necessary to pull of large-scale changes. The company likely tried smaller cultural change efforts along the way which failed, spreading cynicism through the ranks. Communication channels may have completely broken down between large swaths of the organization. Finally, the external pressure to do something quickly may prevent the company from doing it well.

I've experienced this phenomenon firsthand twice in my career.

In the first case, I worked for a technology startup in the heady days of 2000 when nationwide fiber optic networks were being built by a large number of private telecommunications companies seeking to be the first to market. Our team was formed fairly late in the company's life in order to help control costs and improve productivity. Unfortunately, rather expensive cultural behaviors were deeply engrained by that point, and the financial collapse of the company eroded whatever will existed for such efforts. The end came quickly; my tenure lasted less than one year.

My second encounter with failed cultural transformation came with a company that had been in business over a century but only recently transitioned from the active leadership of the founding family, to a trusted consigliere, to a former CFO, to an outsider with a reputation for fundamentally changing failing businesses. Consultants were brought in to both change the culture and help drive projects geared toward generating enough productivity to fund a host of necessary investments. They drew a vision of the new behaviors expected of us, relentlessly reinforced these behaviors and consistently modeled them, all while striving to take as many cash-generating opportunities as our tired brains could spit out and put them on a path to implementation. It was shock and awe on display.

And it failed. Completely.

The causes were legion, but the major contributors were a fragmented leadership team ill equipped to deal with the magnitude of change required and the fact that so few of us even endeavored to help in the effort. We never came close to Gladwell's magic one-third and barely could be said to have Mao's cadres in place. We had the biggest reason for change I have ever seen in that there was a deep love for the company and its history, and the business was failing, yet we never mustered the will to do what we had to do in order to survive.

Transformation strategies require enormous resources, which can be scarce given that they typically occur during times of business hardship when resources are hard to come by. Moreover, they require an immense act of will to stay the course throughout the transformation process. Will can be in short supply when leadership is afraid, or divided, or filled with doubt. Time is the great enemy. Napoleon Bonaparte, no stranger to cultural transformation in times of great tumult, was fond of telling his marshals, "You may ask me for anything you like except time." He was master of Europe then, but another was master of Time.

The advantages of the Transform strategy include:

- The culture is tailored to suit the new needs of the company
- The legacy culture has often been completely discredited
- There is nothing left to lose, often inspiring buy-in for the sake of survival
- Successful transformations make careers

Disadvantages of this approach may include:

- Organizational paralysis
- Precious resources wasted
- May take a long time to effect
- Requires unusual amount of organizational will
- Leadership may be completely unfamiliar with new culture
- Difficult to keep business running while undertaking so massive a change
- External stakeholders with control of resources may lose patience
- Outside expertise is often required
- Employees may utterly reject new culture
- High risk strategy—70% failure rate

The decision as to which strategy to pursue in moving toward your desired company culture from the current model is an important one. The main determinant is how much time and how many resources you can bring to bear on the effort along with how negative the consequences are should you not adopt the new culture. I'd like to offer a final example of a company at this cultural crossroads in order to crystallize this concept still further.

There was a manufacturing plant which was failing and had been slated for closure. The new plant manager, a Lean thinker, requested permission to attempt to implement Lean on a plantwide scale in order to affect a turnaround, which he was given. Over the next several months, all teammates were trained in Lean principles, numerous Kaizen events were held, and the plant's operating metrics blossomed into the best in the company. Lead times dropped, inventory levels nearly evaporated, and the required footprint of the manufacturing operation shrank to the point where the plant manager was able to generate revenue by subletting the space. Quality improved dramatically and rework was nearly non-existent. Employee morale shot through the ceiling.

A happy ending? No.

The plant closed anyway. The decision had already been made. Some of the key personnel involved were relocated to attempt to re-create their successes elsewhere; the rest were left with a life-changing experience and some serious Lean skills. All had to uproot their lives to a significant extent, and all had to leave behind a workplace culture that they had come to truly love, through no fault of their own. Tears were shed and goodbyes bid; the human cost of this endeavor should not be ignored nor diminished. Indeed, the story has stuck with me these decades primarily as a cautionary tale: If we fail to change the culture in time, good people get hurt.

The moral of the story is this: If a cultural transformation isn't successfully undertaken while there is still time on the clock for that business to succeed, it still fails. We can ask for anything we like except time.

EIGHT

Cultural Conformation

"Company cultures are like country cultures. Never try to change one.
Try, instead, to work with what you've got."

—PETER DRUCKER[35]

Why does Peter Drucker believe we should never try to change a company culture?

As we discussed in the last chapter, changing a culture requires a lot of resources, presents a lot of risk, and is inherently disruptive. The more deeply engrained the existing culture is, the more this is true. For this reason, changing any company's culture, especially that level of change we call "transformational," is a high-risk proposition indeed. The juice had better be worth the squeeze.

I learned a hard lesson in cultural change resistance early in my corporate career. I was a member of a new product development team comprised largely of more junior personnel. Our lead project integrator and manufacturing lead were senior to the rest of us and given to lording it over us a bit, habitually showing up late to meetings, bulldozing us, and otherwise making it very clear that they were in charge and we were in servitude.

One day, we were sitting around the conference table waiting for them—again—when we mutually decided we needed a little culture change on the team. The lead project integrator always had to be standing at the whiteboard or flip chart writing things down; it was how he maintained control. The manufacturing lead liked to steer the discussion, constantly interrupting to make his point and derailing any conversation he deemed unworthy. We conspired to change this by deeming one of us to be the recorder and placing all of the markers in front of him. We also named someone the official facilitator and promised to cut off and redirect any and all discussion she didn't initiate.

When our two fearless leaders finally showed up and the meeting began, hilarity ensued. The lead project integrator immediately went to the whiteboard, only to find that an interloper was already standing there with marker in hand. "Have a seat," he said pleasantly, "I've got this."

The lead project integrator cast a confused look toward his partner in crime, who was about to say something when our facilitator interrupted, "Glad you guys could make it. Today we need to discuss the ramp up/ramp down plan. Glenn, how are we looking on that?"

Before Glenn could speak, the manufacturing lead broke in, "What about—?"

"We'll take questions after the discussion," the facilitator replied pleasantly. "Glenn?"

The next 45 minutes were some of the most rewarding of my career. Not only did we have a productive meeting, but we were treated to the spectacle of the increasing discomfort of two people who had been nothing but a thorn in our collective side for months. Time and again they attempted to reassert their prior roles, only to be quickly and politely rebuffed.

I slept the sleep of the just that night.

Then the culture struck back.

Not 48 hours later, our plant manager called us all together and announced he wanted us at the plant at 7 a.m. Saturday. "The team is experiencing some dysfunction," he said, "and we're going to devote the day to fixing it."

Come Saturday morning, my little revolutionary cadre was gathered around the conference table again, waiting for the manufacturing lead and lead project integrator to show up. We were so bored that Glenn started throwing out great questions of pop culture philosophy for our consideration: "Were they called 'The Superfriends' because they were super in and of themselves, or because they were friends of Superman?"

"Well, Aquaman could talk to fish," I offered.

"My aunt talks to fish," Glenn replied, dismissively.

Finally, the guests of honor arrived, and we began an eight-hour ordeal of instruction on teambuilding and drafting plans to improve collegiality among us. Needless to say, the manufacturing lead and lead project integrator took none of the action items.

Our error lay not in bridling under the injustice of a culture that claimed to prize collaboration and boundarylessness but instead rigidly enforced a positional hierarchy and punished anyone who tried to live the culture that had been communicated to us. Rather, we tried to change a deeply entrenched culture with insufficient resources, no real plan, and without thinking through the inevitable forceful response from the agents of the status quo. It really hadn't occurred to us that these two would be so uncomfortable or petty to run to the plant manager with some sad story of insubordination on the project, no doubt imperiling the launch of a multimillion-dollar new revenue stream. We were young and inexperienced; we knew no better.

The smarter play would have been to have gone with the grain of the culture by pursuing a strategy of passive aggression rather than active aggression to get what we wanted. For example, the tardiness issue could have been addressed simply by our vowing not to show up until seven minutes after the meeting began. Why were we late? Busy working on our project deliverables, of course. The punctuality standard couldn't be enforced without the habitually late leadership modeling the behavior, something they were loath to do indeed. For the micromanagement of the meeting, we simply needed to overwhelm them with status updates. The effort to figure out what was meaningful and relevant and what was trivial would have led to their leaving us alone for the most part. Moreover, each of these approaches would have created the appearance that we were in tune with the prevailing culture rather than rebelling against it. As the Chinese master strategist Sun Tzu taught, "The supreme art of war is to subdue the enemy without fighting."[36] Fighting always comes with a nonzero chance of losing.

With this in mind, we recommend the following process in conforming to a culture while simultaneously driving it closer to the desired norms and behavior:

1. **Assess the current culture.** Begin with the dimensional assessment in Chapter 5, which will uncover where the gaps lie. Note which behaviors are present, which need to be removed, and which are not present that need to be. Make a list of each.

2. **Deep-dive on the differences.** As the items on the list represent the major differences between current and desired cultures, we will want to understand how they play out in our culture as deeply as possible. Let's say, for example, that our desired culture requires the Driver of Change to be employees doing their own work, while we currently are driven by external forces. Why should that be so? What prevents our company from actively empowering our teammates?

Is it fear? Inertia? Are there any past change efforts which we could use as case studies to understand how the culture responded and uncover principles for success? Are there any people in the company known for their ability to make change happen despite the cultural resistance they face? What do teammates at various levels think should drive change? Are there any changes they would like to see that are being held back in the current culture? This line of thinking should produce a set of opportunities to magnify the probability of success for driving change within that culture.

3. **Pull the biggest levers.** Our deep dive should have identified the most significant levers for moving the dimension of interest in the direction of our desired culture. Now we must create an innovative strategy to apply pressure to that lever in order to get moving and overcome the inevitable resistance. For example, if our previous investigation determined that one charismatic leader had the magic touch for driving change, we need to get her involved in this effort. Would she be willing to share her secrets with lower-level employees? What if we had them report to her? How do we free her up to be the Chief Change Officer for our company? Think big here; the more force we apply to the biggest levers, the closer we are going to come to our desired culture in an otherwise challenging environment.

4. **Broadcast the results while honoring the present culture.** This is a bit tricky from a communication standpoint. We now have a toehold we can widen and exploit, but to do so we must respect the current culture so as not to appear to be fighting against it. The best example of walking this kind of tightrope is Mark Antony's funeral oration for Caesar, as relayed in Shakespeare's *Julius Caesar*. Antony had been Caesar's second-in-command, a dangerous position to hold given that a group of conspirators from the most highly regarded families in Rome had just murdered Caesar for fear that he would become a dictator. Antony therefore represented the new order that had just been thrown down with great violence by the forces of the status quo, while the Roman people could be expected to side reflexively with those who claimed to have saved the Republic from a tyrant. In the following passage, Antony delivers Caesar's eulogy and, in the process, shows us how to praise a culture while subtly undermining it by awakening a passion for change lurking beneath the surface:

"Friends, Romans, countrymen, lend me your ears;

I come to bury Caesar, not to praise him.

The evil that men do lives after them;

The good is oft interred with their bones;

So let it be with Caesar. The noble Brutus

Hath told you Caesar was ambitious:

If it were so, it was a grievous fault,

And grievously hath Caesar answer'd it.

Here, under leave of Brutus and the rest—

For Brutus is an honourable man;

So are they all, all honourable men—

Come I to speak in Caesar's funeral.

He was my friend, faithful and just to me:

But Brutus says he was ambitious;

And Brutus is an honourable man.

He hath brought many captives home to Rome

Whose ransoms did the general coffers fill:

Did this in Caesar seem ambitious?

When that the poor have cried, Caesar hath wept:

Ambition should be made of sterner stuff:

Yet Brutus says he was ambitious;

And Brutus is an honourable man.

You all did see that on the Lupercal

I thrice presented him a kingly crown,

Which he did thrice refuse: was this ambition?

Yet Brutus says he was ambitious;

And, sure, he is an honourable man.

I speak not to disprove what Brutus spoke,

But here I am to speak what I do know.

You all did love him once, not without cause:

What cause withholds you then, to mourn for him?

O judgment! thou art fled to brutish beasts,

And men have lost their reason. Bear with me;

My heart is in the coffin there with Caesar,

And I must pause till it come back to me."[37]

Note how Antony repeatedly stresses that Brutus, the leader of the assassins, is "honourable," all while raising the question in listeners' minds as to whether he has any honor at all. Honor was clearly a core Roman virtue, a revered aspect of their culture. By invoking it, Antony—himself having the reputation of a dishonorable man since his youth—firmly aligns himself with the values of the Republic and drives a wedge between Brutus and the people. He reminds the Romans of their love for Caesar, who had been the tribune of the common people and was known for his generosity. By the time Antony finishes speaking, the Roman people have turned on Brutus and his fellow conspirators, forcing them to flee the city. This is a highly effective strategy for driving change while conforming to a culture.

5. **Reward new behavior and punish old behavior.** As the new norms take hold, be vigilant in protecting and rewarding those brave souls who first move toward the desired behaviors, recognizing and elevating them, while quietly correcting or removing those who persist in the old behaviors. In our Driver of Change example, we want to make heroes of those employees and their supervisors who make a change to improve their own work or work environment. Note that we want to do this regardless of whether the change is completely successful—we are celebrating the behavior, not the result. I visited a Toyota automotive parts warehouse a few years ago and was impressed that every bay in their large warehouse had been individually customized for the type of material stored within it. Particularly impressive were hinged wooden racks allowing for the vertical storage of exhaust assemblies, which are quite cumbersome and bulky. The manager told me that that was the initiative of one worker who was also a skilled carpenter. He was tired of having to scrap or rework assemblies that were dented due to passing material handling equipment (when laid horizontally, they often stuck outside the bay into the aisle). It had gone through several iterations until the right design had been discovered. "Sometimes the team comes up with some ridiculous ideas," he told me, "but we celebrate them anyway because we know we'll get it right eventually."

Dealing with Blowback

Given the strength of the entrenched culture, it is highly likely that at some point in the conformation strategy execution you will kick over the hornet's nest, even if you are as subtle as Antony was at Caesar's funeral. When faced with threats to its behaviors and norms, the deeply entrenched culture can function as your body's immune system does when it recognizes an infection and fights back hard against the outsiders.

At the outset of any cultural change, the forces supporting the change will be fewer and weaker than those supporting the status quo. These change agents can easily be swept from the field with a little focus and effort from their enemies. The key to avoiding this outcome is similar to that of bacteria in a host: be minimally harmful and avoid detection if at all possible.

If this is not possible, or if the champions of the current culture are already marshaling forces against those seeking change, then a strategy of de-escalation needs to be employed—swiftly. In this situation, the following course of action will be helpful:

1. **Confirm allegiance to the current culture.** Seek opportunities to demonstrate your commitment to the aspects of the current culture that are in harmony with the desired culture. Champion these in word and deed, as publicly as possible. This will counter the narrative that you're a threat to that culture. Limit your deviations from orthodoxy to those dimensions that must change to bring the desired culture into being.

2. **Accentuate the positive.** Rather than take on the inadequacy of the current culture in the areas we need to improve, emphasize the positive aspects of the change. In our Driver of Change example, we want to emphasize how our teammates know their jobs better than anybody and how listening to their improvement ideas would benefit us. Avoid "should" language here in favor of "could" language. "Imagine what we could do if we had 10 people thinking up solutions to this problem instead of one!" Positivity is nonthreatening.

3. **Counterpunch within the culture.** This is tricky but can be devastating: hold the champions of the status quo to their own impossibly high standards of cultural compliance. Expose inconsistencies in how they live the culture wherever possible, but do so subtly. For example, if they are resisting the empowerment of floor-level employees on the basis that they lack information to make good decisions, and the company's culture stresses employee development and growth, you can flip the narrative by embracing the idea of giving these folks

more information. This puts your opponents on the defensive and changes the subject from your deviations from orthodoxy.

4. **Define the path of least resistance.** The reason why bad practices spread virally is that they appear to make someone's job easier. If we want best practices to be adopted, we need to package them up as nicely as possible to make the "What's in It for Me?" apparent to all teammates. Moreover, we must make it easier to adopt the new behavior than to hold on to the old ones. We sometimes get off on the wrong foot with employee empowerment by using Suggestion Boxes, which often involve filling out forms and having to have bureaucratic meetings to follow up on them. This shifts the work to the people with the suggestion, adding to their workload. A better approach would be to capture these ideas at their shift stand-up meeting (which they must attend anyway) or at some meeting where they get something in return for attendance (buy them lunch, pay them for a work hour, etc.). If you want more of something, you need to make it easy to produce.

5. **Recognize that the people are the prize.** While leadership defines culture, culture change is ultimately a battle for the hearts and minds of employees. Understanding what they want and need is crucial to prying their support from the current culture and attaching it to the desired one. In our Driver of Change example, empowering teammates to make changes at their level demonstrates faith in their ability, gives them more control over their day-to-day lives, and builds pride and dignity. It frees supervisors to focus on more strategic issues but can also feel like a loss of power for them. It is therefore wise to give something to supervisors in return for their embrace of the new behavior. Their bonuses could be tied to the percentage of their teams who implement a positive change to their work environment. Special recognition could be given to supervisors demonstrating the most improvement in performance. Additional vacation time could be another incentive, or special giveaways. If supervisors fear accountability for failure of changes that their teams implement, that accountability can be shifted to the lower-level employees or removed altogether.

6. **Objects in motion tend to stay in motion.** Building momentum is key, so preserve forward motion at all costs even if that means slowing down to reduce organizational friction. Check in frequently with stakeholders and trumpet even small wins; the sheer volume will create the perception of movement. Running

meter metrics can be helpful here; a constantly updating ticker showing total number of changes implemented by employees sends the dual message that this change is here to stay, and more and more employees are embracing the new approach.

We're Not Retreating, We're Advancing in Another Direction

What do we do if we've applied the advice above, yet still get overcome by those opposed to this cultural change?

Keep going. Just pick another target.

In our example, we focused on change drivers. Since we have now failed to get all the way to our objective of change being driven by the folks doing the work on the floor, we have a couple of options to consider. We could switch things up by pushing for something which would be an improvement, just not quite as much of an improvement as we ultimately need. What if we focused instead on change driven by management? It may be easier to drive down to the employee level once our managers have gotten a taste of empowerment and incremental change, perhaps naturally through the delegation process.

Alternately, we could elect to focus on another cultural dimension altogether for a while. Then we can return to this one once the furor has died down a bit, or key leaders of the opposition have moved on.

It may be that our timing was simply poor in pushing the initiative when we did. Waiting for a more advantageous time can reap big rewards in the end. The tools provided elsewhere in this book to assess readiness for change can be very helpful in identifying the perfect time to act.

My industrial engineers and I were working in a warehouse where we knew that the way management released orders was contributing greatly to inefficiency and picking errors. Our initial overtures to plant leaders to fix this process fell on deaf ears. We focused on other, smaller problems, slowly building credibility with the team, until the day came when a major customer gave the distribution center manager an earful about getting sent the wrong products, and he brought us out to the floor. "I'm sick of these issues," he told us. "These guys think that part of the problem may be our order release process. Work with them and figure it out before we lose this customer."

That unpredictable event made all the difference in the world in driving positive change in the process. It turned out to be a matter of timing.

Conforming to the culture while making changes to it can be a rewarding strategy provided that great care is taken to always go with the grain of the present culture. It is absolutely crucial to drive change in this scenario under the guise of a consummate insider—someone who eats, sleeps, and breathes the values of the current culture so as not to be marked for removal as an outsider and a threat. If possible, finding a local champion for the necessary changes can significantly increase the chance of success; it will certainly help to assure buy-in over the long term. Maintaining your cool under fire and affecting a positive, upbeat attitude throughout the change process will help as well.

In the end, the key to success will be simple perseverance on the part of those seeking the change. Respecting how deeply engrained current norms and behaviors are within the day-to-day routines of the employee when setting expectations and making implementation plans is very important. Strong cultures change slowly over time and are typically quite resilient to major changes driven by external events unless of the most shocking and extreme magnitude. Change in such an environment tends to happen as a slow drip rather than a raging torrent.

NINE

Cultural Reformation

"History's lesson is to make the most of reform opportunities when they arise because they do not arise often and they do not last long."

—CHRISTOPHER BOND[38]

Reforming a company culture requires even more effort and committed resources than changing certain behaviors and norms within the boundaries of the general culture does. The stakes are higher. Typically, the demand for change from outside and inside factions is much greater than in the previous situation we examined. The gaps between current and desired culture also tend to be larger where reform of the culture is needed. A culture in need of reform is a culture teetering on the precipice—everything may appear to be level, but the slightest movement in the wrong direction may lead to disaster.

Timing is therefore even a more crucial concern when pursuing a reform strategy of cultural change than with a conform strategy. Strike too soon and the organization may not yet be ready to undertake so significant a change as will be required. Wait too long and circumstances may become so dire that the culture change envisioned is no longer sufficient to turn things around.

When is the time ripe for reforming a culture? Look for the following signs:

- The organization has suffered a major setback, such as losing its biggest customer or suffering through a front-page news scandal, which erodes the credibility of the prevailing culture and drives calls for reform.
- Leadership has turned over, opening the organization to a different way of thinking.

- Employees have begun to openly grumble that something is seriously wrong with the company.
- Major layoffs have occurred.
- The company has acquired another company with a radically different culture.
- The company has changed ownership structure from public to private or vice versa.
- The company has missed earnings or the stock price has lost 10% or more of its value recently.
- Company leaders have had to testify to Congress regarding a major negative issue.
- There has been a general degradation in company performance or ethics.
- Tension between employees has risen considerably recently.
- Factions have arisen.
- Employees show signs of distrust in leadership or strategy.
- Employees stop giving feedback.
- Office doors stay closed more often.
- It becomes difficult to get a conference room because employees are huddling in them.
- Hushed conversations in hallways have become the norm.
- Employees generally recognized as highly valued teammates are leaving the company.
- Sarcasm and cynicism become pandemic.

If you see a handful or more of these signs within a company, take heart, my friends, because revolution is in the air. Reform feeds on passionate discontent. There must still be a critical mass of people within the organization who care enough—who hope enough—that they will be willing to make an attempt to correct the current flaws. They cannot be indifferent to the need to do so—no fence-sitters count here. We are talking nothing less than the overthrow of a significant chunk of the culture in place today—and perhaps its champions.

The Challenger space shuttle disaster of 1986 exposed a rotten culture at the National Aerospace and Space Administration. NASA had over the years since the initial development of the space shuttle come to emphasize a "launch at all costs" attitude toward space missions, coveting increased publicity and the funding that came with it. They sought to present shuttle missions as safe and routine endeavors, one more step toward the colonization of space. So confident was Mission Control in its capabilities that it invited a schoolteacher, a civilian, to take part in a Challenger mission. The weather on January 28, 1986, was unusually cold for Cape Canaveral, Florida, a full 20 degrees Fahrenheit colder than the previous low temperature for a shuttle launch. Ice had formed on the orbiter in the freezing temperatures overnight. Engineers raised concerns that the vehicle had never been launched in such cold conditions.

NASA went ahead with the launch anyway.

At 11:39 a.m. Eastern, 17% of Americans, including your author, watched the Challenger disintegrate over the Atlantic Ocean, killing everyone on board.

A government inquiry was assembled to determine what had caused the disaster. Physicist Richard Feynman was part of the panel looking into the disaster, and, during testimony from Morton Thiokol, the company that manufactured the O-rings used to seal shut the segments of the rocket boosters that lifted the orbiter into space, took a sample of the O-ring material, bent it in a clamp, and inserted it into a glass of ice water while he listened to the back-and-forth over whether or not the O-rings were subject to fail at freezing temperatures.

At an appropriate moment, Feynman removed the sample from the glass of ice water and explained that for some seconds after being removed from the clamp it failed to snap back to its former shape, demonstrating to all that the material clearly became less resilient in the cold, compromising its ability to effectively seal a joint. The tone of the investigation changed in that instant from pettifoggery and denial to recognition that NASA ignored concerns raised by its engineers prior to the launch, thereby contributing to the tragic loss of life and the destruction of the space shuttle.

During the ensuing 32 months that the shuttle program was grounded, NASA sought to reform its "launch at all costs" culture. It took nothing less than the worst space disaster in history to bring about this period of self-reflection and reform.

How many of the telltale signs of readiness for reform were apparent at NASA in the wake of that catastrophe?

I'd argue that we could spot: a major setback, employee grumbling, Congressional testimony, general degradation in performance and ethics, heightened tensions, factions (engineers versus leadership), and distrust in leadership or strategy. That's just what was made public; NASA insiders may have witnessed even more of these factors.

You may be ticking these off in your head while reflecting upon the situation at your own company. Below is a simple checklist upon which to record your assessment. The more checkmarks you make, the riper for reform your company is.

While I don't believe firm thresholds to be appropriate in this case (some of these signs are bigger indicators than others), as a general rule, if you have checked off half or more of these items, the situation is very favorable for cultural reform. If you check off nearly all of them, it may be too late for cultural reform to work and should proceed to plan a cultural transformation instead.

Sign	✓
Major organizational failure or setback	
Leadership turnover	
Open employee grumbling	
Major layoffs	
Acquisition of company with very different culture	
Ownership structure change (public to private, private to public)	
Missed earnings or >10% fall in stock price	
Congressional testimony about a company failure	
General degradation in company performance or ethics	
Rising tension between employees	
Employees split into factions	
Employees show signs of distrust in leadership or strategy	
Employees stop giving feedback	
Office doors stay closed more often	
Employees are huddling in conference rooms and offices	
More hushed conversations in hallways	
Employees generally recognized as highly valued teammates are leaving the company	
Sarcasm and cynicism become pandemic	

FIGURE 26. Readiness for cultural reform checklist

You Say You Want a Revolution

Your assessment indicates that the time is right for reforming your company culture. How do we go about doing this? We are going to apply the principles of guerrilla warfare (minus the bullets and bombs, I promise you), which afford key advantages given the asymmetric power at the beginning of the effort between the culture lived today and the desired culture we'll be moving toward.

Now you may be thinking, "C'mon, Veyera, I don't know what kind of knuckle-dragging companies you've worked for, but no way would it ever be so bad at mine that we'd have to look to emulate guerrilla fighters in order to get the job done. Can't my wonderful CEO just hold a town hall meeting and make things happen?"

No, she can't.

What you need to take aboard when undertaking a cultural reform effort is this: if it were easy to get a large organization to stop engaging in one set of behaviors and start adopting another, it would have been done long before the current crisis hit. We are in the mess we are in because humans are creatures of habit and resist change—even good change. Moreover, we are political animals. We often engage in skullduggery to avoid having to make changes we don't wish to make, right down to smiling and nodding when a CEO asks us to do something, knowing full well we're not going to change a thing.

This is not a criticism of people; it is simply how we are wired. I say this as someone who has dedicated his life to getting other folks to embrace positive change.

Indulge if you will one thought experiment to prove this point. Imagine that you're the CEO of an outdoor lifestyle company who has recently lost 100 pounds after becoming a Crossfit fanatic. Your life has changed for the better, exponentially, since you've taken up this fitness regime. Now you've brought your personal trainer to the company and given him a crack staff of additional trainers and a singular mission: transform everyone in the company the way he transformed you. The company's paying for all related expenses and giving employees paid time off to work out.

The question is this: "What percentage of employees will be doing Crossfit one year later if the starting percentage were 10%?"

If you answered anything less than 100%, you recognize that even positive, low-cost change will not be perfectly embraced. If less than 50%, you know that people can stubbornly resist change even under strong peer pressure to change. If less than 10%, you see the world about the same way I do—people resist change for reasons that have nothing at all to do with whether the change is good for them or costs them anything. I believe even some of the people currently on the program will fall away once it becomes free for the simple reason that their skin in the game will have gone down. They may also fear it has become a less elite group. This phenomenon is part of the reason why fitness centers like to sign you up to a yearlong agreement rather than pay-as-you-go. They suspect you'll give up on your workout before the year is up, whereupon they still get paid.

This pernicious resistance to change makes guerrilla warriors of every change agent. I have personally left a meeting with a project approval in hand, strongly endorsed by the CEO and CFO of my company during a meeting with his leadership team wherein he essentially defenestrated the one person to raise an objection ("We'd do this even if it cost us money"), only to have that same person partner up with another member of the leadership team to kill the project dead within two weeks. Nothing material had changed in the interim aside from their ongoing opposition to doing it. This is not an uncommon occurrence in the business world, where politics and ego can bolster natural resistance to change to derail even the most obviously beneficial endeavors.

The following are generally accepted principles of guerrilla warfare.

- The fundamental reality of guerrilla warfare is that it is asymmetrical: the guerrilla forces at the outset of the conflict have far less military power than the forces of the status quo.
- The objective of any conflict involving guerrilla warfare is the hearts and minds of the people.
- The guerrilla relies upon the people for support and sustainment.
- Guerrilla tactics favor mobility and speed; to get bogged down is to risk being surrounded and destroyed by superior forces.
- Surprise is a key success strategy for the guerrilla.
- Guerrillas generally focus on maximizing will over skill.
- Guerrillas typically attack soft targets, especially enemy top leadership.
- Guerrillas do not fight fairly.

For the sake of the developing argument, and to rid ourselves of the historical and political baggage that comes with any discussion of guerrilla warfare, I'm going to recast these slightly into a list of core principles for use in the reformation of company cultures. We'll keep the asymmetrical warfare provenance of these principles strictly between us.

- **Indirect approach.** Due to the current culture being so much stronger than our nascent reform movement, we must avoid direct conflict with it.
- **People focus.** We seek to bond the employees with our desired culture while driving a wedge between them and the current culture. The question we will constantly ask ourselves is: "Will this attract more employees to our cause and/ or alienate them from the current way of doing business?"
- **Collaboration.** We will grow our ranks by inviting the right employees to join us as the reform movement gains steam. It is very important that we continually evolve and avoid top-down leadership of the effort.
- **Opportunism.** We will look for cracks in support for the status quo which we can exploit, open these cracks as wide as it is practical to do so, then move on to the next one.
- **Target influencers.** Victory depends on capturing as many employee influencers as possible in favor of reform while neutralizing or removing as many opponents to reform as possible. We don't need a majority of these but rather one-third.
- **Information.** Having a realistic view of opportunities and our progress is absolutely vital. By maintaining superior information relevant to culture, we will greatly enable the reform movement.

With these more palatable principles in hand, let us now turn to how they are deployed within an effective cultural reform strategy.

How to Win Before Your Opponent Knows There's a Fight: Three Steps to Company Cultural Reform

Winning without fighting is best, as we quoted Sun Tzu earlier. This is as true in business as it is on the battlefield. Conflict wastes resources, breeds dysfunction, and creates lingering wounds which must be healed before the company can move on to better things. In any cultural reform effort, our aim is to win without fighting.

How do we do this? By adopting the following three-step approach.

Step One: Assemble the True Believers

Any successful revolution begins with just a handful of diehards. At one point during the Cuban Revolution, Fidel Castro had just a dozen followers, so few that he was compelled to march them around his mountaintop camp in a circle and have them swap equipment and uniforms when out of sight so as to fool credulous journalists into thinking he had a far larger force at his command. Yet he came to rule Cuba in the end.

We must begin our effort from a similarly humble seed by identifying those hardy souls who we can count upon to fully embrace the change we're seeking.

We'll now introduce the scenario which will take us through the rest of this chapter. Our current culture matches the Engineering archetype (DM – 1, DI – 5, DA – 5, CP – 1, CM – 1, CD – 5), with an elite few responsible for designing work processes, compliance with which is rigidly enforced. We need to move to a Lean culture (DM – 5, DI – 5, DA – 5, CP – 5, CM – 1, CD – 1). The friction points between these archetypes are most marked in the areas of Decision Making (Engineer few, Lean many), Decision-Making Authority—(Engineer hierarchical, Lean credibility-based), and Change Pace (Engineer slow, Lean fast).

Our first challenge then is to find out how many Lean advocates we already have within the organization as these folks can be counted upon to actively support efforts to move the culture in this direction. As we're looking to fly underneath the radar, we aren't just going to send out an e-mail to the All Company distribution list with the subject line, "Who wants to be a Lean guerrilla?" We need to be a bit more subtle than that.

What we'll do instead is create a shadowy front organization for our early activities. We'll call it Wastebusters, and solicit involvement from employees who want to help the company reduce waste. Since waste is the bête noir of Lean thinkers, this net ought to catch a lot of them (along probably with some cost accountants, but we can always throw those back in the pond if need be).[39]

Once our new group starts meeting, we can gather information from them as to the Lean backgrounds of each, then ask members to recommend any other Lean thinkers they know of to take part in this effort. We'll pick a couple of early opportunities to undermine the status quo, which can serve to filter membership and increase focus on just how great Lean is. We'll judiciously avoid playing in any space where those Engineers have a particular interest.

Now that we have our core, we need to swell the ranks a bit before we begin our campaign to erode support for the Engineering culture.

To do this, we'll introduce a tool that we're going to come back to again and again: the stakeholder analysis.

Stakeholder Analysis—the Primary Weapon of the Cultural Guerrilla
Quality practitioners in the audience may be very tempted to flip ahead during this section, familiar as they are with stakeholder analysis. Please don't. There are some new wrinkles in how we apply this method to cultural reform and you'll want to know about them.

Stakeholder analysis is one of the "soft" tools (more qualitative than quantitative) in the process improvement and change management toolkit. The process works like this:

1. Identify stakeholders, which typically means anyone who has an interest in the outcome of a process or product.
2. For each stakeholder, assess current level of support using a standard scale, and put a "__" in the box.
3. For each stakeholder, identify a required level of support using the same scale in order for the effort to be successful, and put a "^" in the box.
4. Where there are gaps between current and desired levels of commitment, develop strategies to close gaps over time, such as:
   a. Communicate. If the reason the commitment level is too low is ignorance of what the change is intended to accomplish, educate the stakeholder.
   b. Co-Opt. Make an ally of the stakeholder by addressing their "What's in It for Me?" concern.
   c. Coerce. If the stakeholder is undermining the effort, it may be appropriate to engage their direct supervisor or a higher-level manager to get them to back off.

Commitment Level	Stakeholders				
	Smith	Jones	O'Rourke	Perez	Huang
Enthusiastic Support – Will work hard to make change happen					
Help It Work – Will lend appropriate support to implement solution	^	^	^ —	^ —	^ —
Compliant – Will do minimum acceptable and try to erode the standard		—			
Hesistant – Holds some reservations; won't volunteer					
Indifferent – Won't help; won't hurt					
Uncooperative – Will have to be prodded					
Opposed – Will openly act on and state opposition to the solution	—				
Hostile – Will block implementation of the solution at all costs					
STRATEGY	Communicate/ Co-Opt	None		None	None

Instructions: For each stakeholder in a given initiative, based on observed behavior (as opposed to statements made), place a "__" in the most applicable Commitment Level row representing their current level of support. Err on the side of lower commitment (less downside risk to initiative). For that same Stakeholder, then place a ^ in the Commitment Level row most closely aligned to the minimum support the initiative requires from them to be successful.

FIGURE 27. Stakeholder analysis example

    d. Collaborate. If "not invented here" is contributing to a stakeholder's lack of support, invite them to help guide the effort.

    e. Corral. If nothing else can be done, fence them off so as to limit their negative impact on the effort

5. Execute the strategies to close the gaps.

Stakeholder analysis is an effective and time-honored method for reducing resistance to change in an organization. To make it even more useful, we're going to tweak the process just a little bit:

1. Identify cultural influencers within the organization (leadership, HR, plus anyone who would be considered either an advocate for the present or desired culture).

2. For each influencer, assess current level of support using a standard scale, and put a "_" in the box.

3. For each influencer, identify a required level of support using the same scale in order for the effort to be successful, and put a "^" in the box.

4. Where there are gaps between current and desired levels of commitment, develop strategies to close gaps over time, such as:

    a. Communicate. If the reason the commitment level is too low is ignorance of what the change is intended to accomplish, educate the stakeholder.

    b. Co-Opt. Make an ally of the stakeholder by addressing their "What's in It for Me?" concern.

    c. Coerce. If the stakeholder is undermining the effort, it may be appropriate to engage their direct supervisor or a higher-level manager to get them to back off.

    d. Collaborate. If "not invented here" is contributing to a stakeholder's lack of support, invite them to help guide the effort.

    e. Corral. If nothing else can be done, fence them off so as to limit their negative impact on the effort.

    f. Collude. Horse-trade support for the new culture against support for something near and dear to the influencer.

    g. Command. If influencer's boss is supportive enough, they may be able to compel their team's support.

    h. Charm. Leverage personal relationships to get influencer to lean forward.

5. Execute the strategies to close the gaps.

In conducting a stakeholder analysis, it is very important to provide a realistic assessment of current and required support levels. This should be based on objective data wherever possible: Watch what influencers do, not what they say. That said, influencers who are baselined in the Help It Work and Enthusiastic Support camps are great fodder for your "true believers." Additional considerations come into play for your inner circle:

- How wide is their sphere of influence? Very senior leaders or extremely popular employees are key.
- Can they be discreet? The recommended strategy requires that the folks driving the reform effort keep quiet about what's going on until success is guaranteed.
- Are they positive? Relentless positivity is essential for the effort, both to persevere during inevitable setbacks and to bolster the morale of others.
- Are they charismatic? Much of the early phase of the strategy requires the ability to connect with people and draw them like a magnet to the cause.
- Are they loyal? This is not a low-risk proposition; should this culture change fail, people could well lose their jobs in the aftermath. We can't afford to have former comrades who are tossing out names of co-conspirators to save their own skins when things get political.
- Do they have influence within key parts of the organization? Someone with C-suite or HR access can be very helpful.
- Do they meld well with the rest of the team? Unity increases the odds of success exponentially.

Once you've settled on the inner circle, bind them together in pursuing the common cause. Stoke dissatisfaction with the status quo among them. Communicate a compelling vision of a better future under the desired culture. Train them on how to communicate that vision to others.

A historical model for this is provided by the Sons of Liberty during the American Revolution, a secret group opposed to the British government and dedicated to lighting the tinder of revolution in the colonies. There were just nine people who formed the nucleus of this supremely influential group when it formed in Boston in 1765 in response to new taxes imposed to recoup the cost of the French and Indian War. If you're familiar with the phrase "no taxation without representation," it is due to their lasting influence. Their tireless efforts and innovative methods to erode support for the government included pamphlet campaigns, tar-and-feathering of loyalists and government officials, and the Boston Tea Party. Much can be accomplished when the right people gather in pursuit of a common objective.

Step Two: Build the Movement

While true believers are terrific assets in cultural reform efforts, you will never have enough of them to carry the day. Their true strength is to act as recruiters and evangelizers for the coming culture. This requires missionary zeal and complete confidence in the righteousness of the cause. It also requires considerable subtlety to avoid attracting negative attention from the vast majority of folks still wed to the status quo.

Recruitment in the early stages should feature the following:

- **One-on-one discussions with influencers.** These should largely be feeling-out discussions to confirm initial stances and generate some sympathy for the cause. Have lunch or coffee with them, away from the office if you can. Continuing our Lean example, a good way to start might be to express disgust for the waste in the business when cash is tight and identify their hot-button issues.
- **Emphasis on building trust.** This is a relationship-building exercise, not a sales pitch.
- **Take a risk.** We tend to like people we take a little risk with. If you get the hint that your target doesn't like their boss, for example, you could make a little joke about them, followed up with "Wait, I shouldn't be telling you that. They're your boss. Whoops!" As long as it doesn't push a hot-button issue with them, a little roguish charm will go a long way.
- **Ask them to do you a favor.** That's right—they are to do a favor for you, not the other way around. It turns out that we like people we do something for even more than those who've done something for us. It builds relationships.
- **Listen more than you talk.** You're probing for intelligence here; you can't do that while talking too much.
- **Aim for the heart.** Figure out what they love, then align the discussion to ensure that the desired culture will look like it. For example, if you're talking

with a stressed-out production manager who can't get a moment's peace, talking about how calm and peaceful that shop floor was at the Toyota plant may look very good in comparison to their day-to-day experience in the current culture.

- **Make the overture.** Once the relationship has been fully established over several discussions, ask them if they would be willing to help you actually do something about what you've been discussing. Make it clear that you admire them and believe that they could be key to turning shared desires for culture change into a reality. If they seem lukewarm, back away immediately. "Yeah, probably a dumb idea. Who do you think will win the French Open this year?"

Growing your forces at this point will require a lot of retail networking. The sheer repetition of these discussions will hone your message and bind the inner circle together as you become ever more effective proselytizers for the new culture.

Think about this part of the effort as building up an appetite for the new culture among those destined to be its early adopters. It is a time for discernment and soft probing for nascent support for what we hope to achieve. Subtle influencing during this stage can be very helpful as well.

How big must the movement be for this stage to be successful? If the tipping point per Malcolm Gladwell is about 33%, targeting 10% of the population during this phase would not be out of bounds, presuming that number can be effectively managed by the inner circle of the reform movement. Time being the enemy, the ceiling on recruitment during this phase may be determined by the clock rather than the proportion. It is better generally to get moving once you've got a critical mass of change agents than to wait for larger numbers before taking action. Once support for the status quo begins to erode, people will begin to flock to the reform banner.

Step Three: Undermine the Status Quo

Shortly after we've reached critical mass in the size of the movement, it will be time to act. We must erode support for the current culture and begin our battle for the hearts and minds of the people of our company. At first, skirmishes will be very minor and even of questionable value. Over time, the tempo will increase along with the magnitude of the attacks on the current culture, much like a frog slowly boiled in a pot will see the waters around him go from cool and placid to turbulent and steaming.

In our Lean scenario, we must overcome an Engineering culture whereby a few highly skilled employees dictate the work of the rest. We are going to assess our enemies' strengths and weaknesses prior to choosing targets to attack.

SWOT analysis is a terrific tool employed by process improvement professionals to ensure they have a clear view of the environment in which positive changes will be implemented. The lens we will be using on this will be "... relative to our desired culture"; in other words, this will be a comparative analysis. As a reminder, Strengths refers to intrinsic positives associated with the subject; Weaknesses are intrinsic negatives. Opportunities are external positives which could be gained; Threats are external negatives which may apply in the future. The left side of Figure 28 will therefore have the character of what an avatar of our new culture would like about the old; the right what they would dislike about it. Working with our true believers, we determine the following regarding the Engineering culture:

STRENGTHS	WEAKNESSES
• Data-driven decision-making • Focus on designing processes • Deliberate in action	• Employees are not empowered • Hierarchical decision-making • Highly resistant to change • Externally motivated to change • Slow to action • Lack of people skills
OPPORTUNITIES	THREATS
• Focus resources on designing for big wins • Outsource non-engineering functions	• Micromanagement • Disgruntled employees • Obsolescence • Apathy • Change bottlenecks • Unpopular bureaucracy

FIGURE 28. Current culture SWOT analysis

In a move that will delight any Machiavellians in the audience, we are going to use the Threats quadrant in order to attack the Weaknesses of the current culture, while keeping a watchful eye on our adversaries' seizing of Opportunities. This

Strategy	Tactics
Fan the flames of discontent.	• Track and publicize how long it takes to get approvals for minor changes. • Support employee suggestions and recommend they ask their supervisors to implement. • Bombard approvers with suggestions that will be popular with lower-level employees. • Provide a listening ear for anyone with a complaint about the current culture. • Ask questions in public forums which call attention to shortcomings of current culture.
Idealize the alternative.	• Organize a tour of a company with the desired culture. • Bring in lunch speakers to advocate for positive aspects of desired culture. • Buy copies of books related to desired culture and leave in strategic locations. • Have someone on the team model the desired behavior, plant fellow supporters, and ostentatiously praise that person for their behavior in front of others. • Talk key aspects of the new culture up with anyone suffering from or complaining about the corresponding aspect of the current culture. • Rally around charismatic leaders who can model the new behaviors and show the way.
Denigrate the current culture.	• Associate the current culture everywhere with "the past." • Gently mock ridiculous aspects of the current culture. • Give silly nicknames to heroes of the current culture. • Magnify defects of the current culture. • Ensure that stories about cultural failures get widely spread. • Create a meme for why the current culture isn't suitable and circulate it. • Leverage the "slippery slope" by disobeying the more questionable requirements of the current culture en masse. • Target key influencers to defect.

FIGURE 29. Cultural change preparation strategy

will erode the legitimacy of the present culture and increase the attractiveness of the new culture and begin to shift the population our way.

Your aim is to roll a snowball downhill and create an avalanche over time, while ensuring that no one knows who rolled the snowball. When the current culture is being openly ridiculed with impunity, it will be time for the next step.

Step Four: Look for or Manufacture a Crisis

Timing is important in launching revolutions. But how do we pick the best time to light all the tinder we have been placing around the old culture?

We look for a crisis, by which I mean a culminating event that can be used to pivot from the old culture to the new one. We have the solution in hand; we're merely waiting for the problem to become manifest.

I shared the example earlier of how my team and I finally came to be allowed to fix a warehouses order release process. In that case, the prospect of losing a big customer triggered a crisis in which a leader previously wed to the old way of doing things demanded we implement ours.

We know that building a Lean culture is extremely important to our company's future. We just need some way to demonstrate to that crucial third of employees that this is the case. We've been stoking the flames for quite some time now, building resentment against our current sclerotic and elitist culture while creating a genuine hunger to empower employees and make some much-needed changes to reduce waste and improve the financial situation of the company. What we need now is The Last Straw, the one event that will signal the arrival of our new Lean way of operating.

This could be the loss of a customer due to our slowness to take action. It could be a beloved employee leaving the company because they're fed up with not being able to make reasonable changes to how they work. It could be an overreaction on the part of the current culture to some minor act of disobedience or mockery. It could be a scandal.

In the end, it doesn't really matter, because it's simply a predicate for the moment we stand up and say, "Enough! Here's what we ought to do about this."

A Lean leader I knew used the crisis occasioned by the selling of his company to another to drive the culture in the right direction. He told me, "If you don't have a crisis, manufacture one!" by which he meant that having some sort of major cause of anxiety and fear turned out to be a great motivator to try something new. It breaks the old habits quickly. "Nothing so concentrates the mind as knowing you'll be hanged in the morning," as the old saying goes.

When enough employees have had enough about something, action will follow.

The Boston Massacre, which kicked off the American Revolution, began when, after months of disgruntlement over the lodging of British soldiers with area families against their will, one man asked a soldier passing by. "Soldier, will you work?" he yelled. "Aye!" came the response, whereupon the citizen made a vulgar suggestion regarding a particularly demeaning task regarding an outhouse. The soldier's retaliation drew a crowd, which drew more Redcoats, followed by someone yelling "Fire!" (We don't know whom.) The man mocking the soldier triggered a tragedy that day, one which would ultimately earn the American colonists their liberty. (Please don't kick off your crisis by yelling "Fire!")

In our Lean example, the crisis could come from losing in the marketplace due to excessive lead time, or problems with excess inventory, or the madness of overproduction to fill warehouses with finished goods that won't be needed for months, if ever. It could be caused by a cash crunch, or layoffs, or plant closures, or even the need to move to weekend or third-shift production schedules due to insufficient throughput. It is not important that the crisis be as big a threat as presented; it is vital that the crisis be plausible. Implausible crises simply erode the credibility of the person warning about them.

Whatever the cause, make sure someone representing the Lean culture is present to offer up the solution at just the right time.

Step Five: Win and Keep Winning

Put your best and brightest on resolving this first problem. This will increase credibility, build momentum, and raise morale to a fever pitch. Be humble and keep expectations low, then deliver in excess of those expectations. In the event of a setback, scapegoat the old culture and move swiftly to tackle another problem.

When you get a win, celebrate it. Loudly. Be gracious toward former adversaries and invite them to join the party; this will both increase your ranks and decrease those of the last holdouts. Reward your allies prodigiously.

This is not to say that there won't be speed bumps along the way. There always will be. But once the new culture has been tried and seen some successes, it will feel shiny and new to most people, something more interesting than the old way of doing things.

At that moment, the old culture is dead.

Long live the new culture!

Once past the tipping point, you can at last be overt and take advantage of the company's institutions and processes directly in the promulgation of the new culture. This may include:

- Training
- Communications
- Staffing
- Project management
- Budgets
- Strategy

Avail yourself of these spoils of war. You'll need them to sustain the gains already made and to achieve formal recognition of the new culture as the only legitimate one for the company.

The Empire Strikes Back

All of that sounds nice enough, but what happens if the ancien régime doesn't just wither away in the face of the desired culture's triumph? What if they dig in and continue to fight back, or even worse, read this book and start fighting guerrilla-style themselves?

First, once people start moving, inertia works for you—it's hard to stop them, much less get them to move back in the opposite direction. Counterrevolutions rarely succeed historically for this reason. Generally you would have to make a pretty terrible mistake in order to scare the company back onto a path which was already failing.

Second, such a counterrevolution would require even more resources and sustained effort than the original reform movement did, resources and effort you are now using to pursue the priorities of the desired culture. Absent an infusion of cash, people, and support from credible leadership, this simply will not happen.

Third, even in the unlikely event of a complete scorched-earth retaliatory campaign from vanquished prior leadership (think of something like a shareholder revolt, or hostile acquisition, or maybe the owner of a private company electing in a fit of anger to shutter the doors), you still have options. The first is to generate sufficient early successes with the desired culture so as to bolster support. People generally do not like to mess with success, even where egos get involved. The second is to take advantage of your new position as an insider to thwart efforts to peel away your support. Companies that have successfully resisted calls from their workforce to form labor unions have usually done so by removing or ameliorating the biggest irritants to workers while giving them more of what they value, whether that is higher wages, better working conditions, more job security, and so on. Sufficient attention to the needs of your people does much to inoculate your nascent culture against nasty bugs introduced by the hostile world outside.

In short, stay the course and keep leveraging the strengths of the desired culture. As it enables the company to better accomplish what it needs to accomplish, you cannot help but be more successful than the culture you've replaced in the near-to-mid future.

Should it prove otherwise, it may be time for more reform. . . .

TEN

Cultural Transformation

"There is nothing more difficult to take in hand, more perilous to conduct, or more uncertain in its success, than to take the lead in the introduction of a new order of things."

—NICCOLO MACHIAVELLI[40]

The reader may be forgiven for wondering, given the amount of effort and drama involved in reforming a company culture, whether wholly transforming one is ever advisable, even if such a thing were remotely possible. Machiavelli shares our trepidation, as demonstrated by the quote above. The *ne plus ultra* of culture change is transformation. Nothing is undertaken with greater fear of failure; there is no riskier endeavor; and the 30% success rate means that all that effort and risk-taking will go for naught more than two-thirds of the time. This is not an undertaking for the faint of heart.

So why attempt to transform a culture at all?

Because we simply have no other choice.

A company's culture is nothing more than a tool allowing the firm to do what it must do. If the current tool is completely unsuitable for the task and cannot be sufficiently improved, we have no alternative but to employ a new one. The company itself will fail if the culture doesn't change.

Humans being human, we resist change until it is absolutely necessary. By that point, the company is usually in crisis, the negative results of a mismatch between current culture and needed culture having so compromised the effectiveness and efficiency of the organization that it is in imminent danger of catastrophic failure. In this regard, companies are rather like fancy sports cars. If the owner refuses to change the oil at the same time they begin entering races, the situation will degrade steadily over time. At first, the car's performance will noticeably drop. At this point, the owner could make a slight change by adding oil (a Conform strategy), and the negative consequences might well evaporate entirely for a time. If they persist with the current "no maintenance" culture, however, eventually the motor temperature will creep up to the danger level due to lack of lubrication and running harder due to the performance drop. The owner could still adopt a Reform strategy—add liquid cooling to the engine to get the temperature down. Persist on this path and the engine will seize unless you fundamentally rethink this strategy and start changing your oil like everyone else. Once the engine has seized, the race is over.

Companies in need of cultural transformation are therefore nearly always in a state of disarray and despair. The market is in the process of rejecting their products and services, with disastrous impact to revenue and margins. Inventories rise. Plants either overproduce to use capacity or begin downsizing in the face of diminished demand. Purchasing power erodes with demand, driving prices up. If layoffs have occurred, labor costs will rise with buyouts and retention bonuses. This combination of diminishing revenue and rising costs creates cash crunches, which in turn drive down investment in areas previously considered essential such as maintenance, dividend payouts, bonuses, paying suppliers on time, and the like. This of course mortgages the future, and if conditions persist, the cost of deferring such payments will have serious consequences down the road. For publicly traded companies, earnings often get missed in these scenarios, pummeling the stock price and eroding confidence in leadership by the board and financial sector. Both publicly and privately held companies will have to pay more for credit, making it more difficult to remain liquid.

This financial and operational death spiral will accelerate until either market conditions fundamentally change or the company does. Aside from a white-knight investor stepping in or the sudden demise of the competition, it is hard to envision a scenario where the cultural misalignment doesn't require a transformation effort. If your company is in this death spiral, you won't want to adopt a "hope for favorable winds" strategy in any case; these are low-probability events. As a result of the crisis and the scarcity of available resources and the devastating blow to morale which follow in its wake, viable solutions become "highly constrained" in Engineering Speak—we don't have many good options left. Moreover, key stakeholders begin checking out, either by leaving the organization or by resigning themselves to the inevitable demise of the enterprise. The usual inertia that drives so much resistance to change approaches paralysis.

Optimists will note that recognition of the problem and the burning platform for change shouldn't be a problem in this case, but that simply isn't true. The refusal of leadership to drive significant cultural change to this point leads to a fair portion of the company living in denial. I've seen companies where field personnel literally scoffed when a midlevel manager from headquarters tried to explain the dire market situation to them, even after they had seen for themselves the loss of top customers and layoffs. As far as they were concerned, this was simply a momentary dip—things would get better soon.

Part of the problem is that leadership tends to be loquacious in good times and laconic in bad; we like to trumpet the positive while muting the negative. This divides the company more distinctly into insiders and outsiders. When a dotcom company I worked for began to flounder, I noticed that doors to offices in the Finance area which had previously been wide open most of the time were now closed nearly all of the time, a clear indicator that they were working with information they didn't want prying eyes outside of the team to see. Meanwhile, leadership maintained that all was well. This deceit, however well intentioned, erodes the credibility of leadership and the trust between teammates.

That is the situation most companies find themselves in when cultural transformation is finally placed on the table: desperate, dysfunctional, and on the cusp of bankruptcy. Transforming a company culture is an option only when virtually all alternatives have failed or been rejected.

Given this reality, a checklist for cultural transformation readiness may seem like overkill. Some companies may be better at hiding severe issues from the rank and file than others; if so, the checklist below may prove useful in connecting the dots and realizing that the time has come for a sweeping effort to replace the current culture.

As with the checklist for cultural reformation, the more checks in the boxes here, the more ripe the company is to transform the culture. If you've checked 75% or more of the boxes, it may be too late to right the ship and will take an extraordinary effort (and no small amount of luck) to turn the situation around.

Sign	✓
Major organizational failure or setback	
Senior leadership turnover	
Shouting matches or physical altercations between employees	
Major layoffs—multiple rounds	
Acquisition of company by a larger company	
Closing of facilities and/or selling off of divisions	
Missed earnings or >25% fall in stock price	
Congressional testimony about a company failure	
Company moves into unprofitability and/or starts taking on debt	
Rising tension between leaders	
Leadership split into factions	
Attendance at mandatory functions drops	
Leadership avoids employees	
Office doors stay closed more often	
Employees are doing less and less work	
Open conversations in hallways regarding job hunts and bankruptcy	
Company credit rating gets downgraded to near-junk status	
Consultants show up en masse	
Employees at all levels are leaving the company	
Apathy becomes pandemic	

FIGURE 30. Readiness for cultural transformation checklist

Congratulations! I'm Sorry

Your company leadership has finally seen the light and recognizes that changing the company's culture is the most important challenge to be undertaken. Moreover, you have been tapped to lead the transformation effort. Congratulations!

The responsibility to save the company and build a brighter future for all now falls directly on your shoulders. You'll need to figure out what you need to do it, how to get those scarce resources, how to motivate people who may already have a dress picked out for the company's funeral, how to partner with some of the very people who created the current crisis, and how to survive being a lightning rod for a change most people never wanted to happen in the first place. By the way, you might have a one in three chance of succeeding. I'm sorry.

The first thing you must do is take some steps to protect yourself. Regardless of how this effort turns out, your career will continue. If leadership is going to ask you to take on such a high-risk endeavor, it is your duty to request and get assurances that will mitigate your personal risk. Culture change is not a suicide mission.

I recommend asking for the following. You may be willing to settle for a small portion of this list, but would be wise to obtain all you can:

- Leadership support
  - **Senior title.** As you will be dealing with different factions of the leadership team and need equal authority, your title should match those of the top leader's direct reports. If there's a C-suite, you should be Chief Transformation Officer or Chief Culture Officer. If the model features senior vice presidents, you should be Senior Vice President of Culture. Titles matter, both during the effort and to communicate the scope of your responsibilities in your résumé later.
  - **Geographic scope.** You should have this responsibility company-wide, for all locations. You cannot survive with separate cultures.
  - **Reporting structure.** You report directly to the CEO/president. There is no alternative. You need ready, immediate access to the top person in the company when you run into the inevitable resistance to change. If you do not get this item, do not take the job. It is doomed to failure without this.
  - **Budget and staff approval.** No one should be in the approval line except for the CEO/president.
  - **Board of Directors access.** For publicly traded companies, you need to attend board meetings and to present to the board when you see fit. This is another crucial item. A disconnect between the president/CEO and the board will doom the effort. Moreover, the board is often weighted with stakeholders in the culture, former founders and senior leaders as well as institutional and industry key players. They need to know what you're doing and why, and you need to know what advice they're giving senior leadership.
  - **Leadership team access.** You are to be a part of the senior leadership team and included in all meetings. This provides an effective vehicle for communication as well as a strong message that you are not to be ignored.

— **Office.** Your desk should either be adjacent to the CEO/president's office or even within it. This is an intensive effort which requires constant, immediate access to the top decision-maker in the company. This will no doubt upset whomever's spot you take, particularly when they notice you spend little physical time at your desk because you're so busy making change happen. It is another indication of the importance of your mission and the unwavering support from the top. If you absolutely cannot get this, then wherever your office is needs to be the hub for the effort: All leaders (even the CEO) need to come to you.

— **Cell phone.** Every senior leader needs to have your cell phone in their contacts list and the norm established that when you call, they must take the call immediately. The presumption must be that if you're calling, it is an emergency call and automatically has the highest priority.

— **Conference rooms.** You will have at least two reserved for your use at all times. This includes remote sites during windows of time which you will define. One will be the war room where your team will primarily work. The other will be for meetings. This is another required perk that will no doubt outrage the status-seekers in the organization, and which is why you must do it.

— **Meeting attendance.** If you call a meeting, attendance is mandatory. Period. The first time anyone elects to attend another, the CEO/president needs to land on them like a grand piano to the point of terminating their employment. This effort is about the very survival of the company; there is literally nothing more important than the transformation. Never reschedule a meeting to suit an attendee's schedule; don't even look at their calendar. This train *must* run on time.

— **Decision-making authority.** The senior leadership team will often be informed of decisions, not invited to weigh in on them. This is necessary because some portion of the team will often be opposed to the transformation effort and either passive-aggressively or openly attempt to derail it. Decisions will either be communicated by the top person or by yourself. This will be a tough pill to swallow for companies that prize collaboration, but sinking ships cannot operate by consensus.

— **Degree Absolute.**[41] In the event of persistent, implacable opposition from anyone in the company, you must have an understanding with the CEO/

president that he will either terminate the employment of that employee or honor your resignation.

- Insurance against failure
  - CEO/president must sign an agreement to the effect that you are to be indemnified against the prospect of the effort not succeeding (an exception for specific gross misconduct on your part is acceptable) to include:
    - Fully guaranteed salary for a defined time period that will be paid to you even if the effort or company fails prior to that date; in other words, if the company elects to halt the effort, you get paid as though they'd continued
    - Strongly positive recommendation regarding your work to be final-edited by you and signed by CEO/president
    - Agreement not to disparage
    - Bonus, stock options, pension, 401(k) match, and any other previously agreed upon financial benefits to be fully honored without regard to success or failure of effort or company
    - No noncompetition clause unless salary and other benefits continue for full term of clause
    - Healthcare and other benefits continue as though you remained an employee
    - Outplacement services with reputable company to be paid for by company for 18 months following end of engagement
    - No contesting government unemployment benefits
- Resources
  - Project team
    - Any current company personnel selected shall be detailed to transformation effort for the duration at your discretion.
    - Any outside personnel required will be hired/fired at your discretion.
    - Typical roles required—
      - Project manager
      - Finance analyst
      - Trainer
      - Data analyst
      - Communications specialist
      - HR specialist

- ▪ Engineer
- ▪ Operations expert
- ▪ Facilitator
- ▪ Quality expert
- ▪ Lean expert
- ▪ Six Sigma Master Black Belt
- — Budget
  - • Funds as requested with approval by CEO/president only
- — Timeline
  - • 18–24 months would be standard request
  - • In the event crisis drives earlier completion, budget and team resources committed must increase

The initial inclination when presented with such a list may be to view it as excessive or even unprecedented. The reality is that a company situation's in a transformation scenario is usually so severe that absent exceptional commitment, the company will likely fail. Honoring these requests comes at less cost than the failure of the company, which will usually ruin the finances of many employees, destroy the reputation of senior leaders, and wipe out shareholders. You or I might be relied upon to balk at "excessive" hospital costs until our very lives depended upon the healthcare we receive, at which point no price is too high.

None of the items in the list above were included arbitrarily, but rather to induce the organization and the change agent to put forth the best possible effort with the greatest probability of success. By seeking and obtaining such power and resources, we are in fact betting on a successful outcome. Most efforts that fail do so because the people charged with making them happen lack the authority, resources, or courage to pursue the effort all the way to victory. Another Winston Churchill quote leaps to mind:

> "I say to the House as I said to the ministers who have joined this government, I have nothing to offer but blood, toil, tears, and sweat. We have before us an ordeal of the most grievous kind. We have before us many months of struggle and suffering.
>
> "You ask, 'What is our policy?' I say it is to wage war by land, sea, and air. War with all our might and with all the strength God has given us, and

to wage war against a monstrous tyranny never surpassed in the dark and lamentable catalogue of human crime. That is our policy.

"You ask, 'What is our aim?' I can answer in one word. It is victory. Victory at all costs—Victory in spite of all terrors—Victory, no matter how long and hard the road may be, for without victory there is no survival.

"Let that be realized. No survival for the British Empire, no survival for all that the British Empire has stood for, no survival for the urge, the impulse of the ages, that mankind shall move forward toward His goal.

"I take up my task in buoyancy and hope. I feel sure that our cause will not be suffered to fail among men. I feel entitled at this juncture, at this time, to claim the aid of all and to say, 'Come then, let us go forward together with our united strength.'"[42]

At the time Churchill delivered this speech, Great Britain was in a crisis far worse than anything our companies might face: surrounded by implacable foes, with few allies, and with little prospect of turning back the tide of Axis triumph. Yet the sentiments he expressed apply as well to the situation a company desperately needing cultural transformation as they did to darkest days of the Second World War.

Churchill prevailed. And so can we.

When you are asked to lead such a dramatic transformation, make no mistake: you are your company's Churchill. And as Churchill elsewhere said, "Give us the tools and we'll finish the job."[43]

Step One: Assemble the Transformation Team

Initial assurances in place, we now undertake the vital task of building the finest team possible to begin the transformation of our culture. While this will be a similar exercise in several ways to that we undertook for reforming a culture, it will differ in terms of the intensity of the effort and the fact that this team must work in a completely seamless fashion. You should consider the following when putting together this team:

- **Known quantities.** There will be very little time for the normal team evolution in a transformation effort. You need to have people who know each other, like or at least respect each other, and work well together. This will be a high-stress engagement; we cannot afford to have it derailed by personality conflicts or teammates who cannot handle the sustained intensity of it. Moreover, they should be completely reliable in terms of pursuing the goal.

- **Influencers.** Anyone chosen for the team needs to be an exceptional influencer, able to turn employees in a positive direction even on the very worst day of their lives. You can pull technical skills from other quarters, but anyone within the inner circle needs to be terrific at motivating people. If they are an insider, they need to be plugged into all major networks at the company and popular and charismatic enough that they can pull a significant part of the company along with them simply by visibly supporting the effort.

- **Experts.** Transformations are fiendishly difficult efforts. Much of the team needs to be comprised of people who are absolutely at the top of their game professionally and possessing terrific judgment from having previously tackled some of the biggest and most complex business problems to be found. This is not the time to learn on the job. For this reason, the team will tend to skew older. You want the average experience level to be on the order of 20–25 years of relevant business experience.

- **Doers, not dialers.** Doers do; dialers call someone who does. You need people willing to roll up their sleeves and work alongside the employees of the company. When following the failure of his Dardanelles campaign during the Great War, Winston Churchill, First Lord of the Admiralty, lost his post, he didn't sit the war out but rather fought in the trenches as a lieutenant colonel, risking his own life to get his hands dirty in that deadly conflict. That is the spirit we need in a transformational effort.

- **High integrity.** You need good, honest people who will not place their agenda above that of the team or company. The first time someone gets caught padding expenses, the whole effort will lose credibility. People who oppose the change effort or simply don't like being brushed aside so the transformation team can do their jobs will seek to exploit any misconduct, no matter how minor. You need people you can trust to do the right thing even when you're not looking.

- **High energy.** This effort is going to be a marathon. You need people who can run that marathon while smiling. Workaholics catch a lot of flak, sometimes for the lack of balance in their lives, but they are precisely the sort of people needed in this type of project. Expect 12–16–hour days, 6–7 days a week, for two years. This is the equivalent of a long military deployment.

- **Homers.** If your team is flying in and out of town all the time, you're going to drop productivity by over 40% for the simple reason that they will lose a full day each week (a half day Monday, a half day Friday) due to travel plus the weekend spent at home. That leaves just four days per week of actual working time. That is not likely to be sufficient to drive the necessary change within the required period of time. You need people who are going to stick around all week until the job is done.

- **Doubting Thomas.** You need one—and only one—skeptic on the team, preferably someone with a long history with the current culture who can help you understand where the obstacles to change are. This skeptic needs to completely buy in to the need for the change and be deeply invested in making it happen. They are the "inside person" for pulling off the heist. They must be absolutely loyal and trustworthy. They serve as scout and guide, and are there to demolish groupthink.

- **Bare-knuckle fighters.** There will be a point, sometimes more than one, in these transformation efforts when things get a bit chippy. People reach their limits. When the stress level is high enough, when the fear is palpable, when they feel like what they have spent most of their careers doing is being discarded by a bunch of arrogant short-timers profiteering from the misery of their beloved company, they will push back. Violently. You need people who are watchful for this and who can back them down with brutal efficiency. This is not a role for people who are afraid of conflict.

- **Humble.** Given the above, this is going to be the counterintuitive characteristic. Arrogant people do dumb things when situations turn bad, mainly in a misguided effort to save their pride. The humble person will recognize the magnitude of the challenge before them, understand that when you take on a mountain, the mountain sometimes wins, and be okay with that. They do not get so caught up in the high drama of the cultural transformation that their self-worth dies with it should it fail. Every great general, every great business leader, every great athlete, loses sometimes. It is how they deal with the inevitable downturn which defines their greatness in the end. Choose people who believe in the team and believe in themselves, but who do not believe in their own divinity.

That is a lot of requirements. You may be wondering if all of those attributes may be found in a small group of people, particularly if they must be found quickly. They can. They will. But you can drastically increase the odds of success if you get in the habit of always having your Dream Team written down on a small slip of paper in your wallet and stay in contact with them. Even if you're not driving the transformation train, whoever is may welcome a group of top professionals you vouch for.

Be prepared to pay them well. Folks like this don't come cheaply, and they are almost always going to have to be lured away from other important and well-paid work. Be reasonable and you'll get them aboard. After all, it's not every day that you get invited to save the world.

Step Two: Understand the Current Situation

With the A-team in place, including in all likelihood a number of folks unfamiliar with the company and the situation in which it has found itself, we need to inquire deeply into the current situation and how it came to be that way. This is needed both to get a common vision for the team as well as to test key assumptions made at the outset of the effort. If success proves to be well nigh impossible, this is also the time to walk away.

We approach this phase of the transformation effort much as one would approach due diligence data-gathering of a potential acquisition target. Answering the following questions will help, although you will certainly want to revise and extend this questionnaire to suit the specific transformation scenarios you encounter.

Answering these questions with the help of senior leadership is a good start, but that represents insider opinion, not objective reality. You will need to test the answers to these questions against objective reality as well as the opinions of outsiders and lower-level employees to get a true picture of what is going on. It should be no surprise that in companies in crisis, leadership often has a very different view of reality than the rest of the company, and quite often an erroneous one.

The first several weeks of the engagement needs to be spent creating an accurate picture of the situation and either a confirmation that the desired culture will align fully with the new company strategy or a new desired culture will be chosen.

Company Current State Questionnaire

Financial

1. What is the current financial condition of the company?

2. Where is the company's financial condition expected to be in the next 24 months?

3. What options aside from this transformation are being considered to improve the financial stability of the company?

4. What is the earliest date by which these options would be implemented?

5. What is the current level of risk of the company being acquired? Over what time horizon?

Organizational

6. How many employees does the company have?

7. What is the organizational structure of the company?

8. Who is the leadership team? What changes are currently being contemplated with regard to the leadership team? Who is at risk of leaving?

9. What sites does the company operate out of?

10. What organizational changes are being considered in light of the current company situation? What is the earliest date by which these would be implemented?

Strategic

11. What is the company's purpose?

12. What is the company's current strategy?

13. Why is the company in crisis?

14. What is the company seeking to do in the future?

15. What is the biggest risk to successfully executing the strategy?

Cultural

16. What is the state of the company culture today?

17. What aspects of the culture are holding the company back in the move to execute the new strategy?

18. How do employees view the current culture?

19. How did the current company culture come about?

20. What parts of the organization will have the biggest issues with culture change?

FIGURE 31. Current state of the company questionnaire

Step Three: Defy the Old Culture

With the team in place and the course of action clear, it is time to get moving. Unlike a cultural reformation effort where we seek to fly beneath the radar and build up momentum over time, a cultural transformation begins with a big bang. In one fell swoop, we must utterly discredit the old culture, crisply define the new culture, instill hope in the audience that this effort will succeed, and introduce the team to make it happen. Accomplishing this will immediately put defenders of the status quo on their heels and lend momentum to those looking for a change. This is high-stakes drama to be certain.

Louis V. Gerstner, Jr. took over IBM at a point where industry insiders and no small proportion of the company's leadership felt that the tech giant ought to be broken up into separate parts and sold off. He felt that the company could work if only it could change its culture from the ossified bureaucracy it had become to the customer-focused, problem-solving engine it could be. Change needed to occur quickly and decisively. In his memoir, *Who Says Elephants Can't Dance?*, Gerstner relays how he got the ball rolling in his very first meeting:

"One of the first meetings I asked for was briefing on the state of the [mainframe computer] business. I remember at least two things about that first meeting with Nick Donofrio, who was then running the System/390 business. One is that I . . . experienced a repeat of my first day on the job. Once again, I found myself lacking a badge to open the doors at the complex, which housed the staffs of all of IBM'S major product groups, and nobody there knew who I was. I finally persuaded a kind soul to let me in, found Nick, and we got started. Sort of.

"At that time, the standard format of any important IBM meeting was a presentation using overhead projectors and graphics that IBMers called 'foils' [projected transparencies]. Nick was on his second foil when I stepped to the table and, as politely as I could in front of his team, switched off the projector. After a long moment of awkward silence, I simply said, 'Let's just talk about your business.'

"I mention this episode because it had an unintended, but terribly powerful ripple effect. By that afternoon an e-mail about my hitting the Off button on the overhead projector was crisscrossing the world. Talk about consternation! It was as if the President of the United States had banned the use of English at White House meetings."[44]

In one action—standing up, walking over to the projector, and switching it off—Gerstner sent a clear message that he was there to fundamentally change the culture. It is hard for people today to understand just how important that endless procession of "foils" was to IBM. I worked with a group of folks whose IBM circuit card manufacturing plant had been purchased by a Japanese company several years before yet still operated on the IBM template of big, thick stacks of overhead slides hammered at customers until we begged for the sweet release of a bathroom break. It was not simply how they prepared for and ran meetings, but it was how they thought. Gerstner coming in from a snack biscuit company and turning off that slide projector was equivalent to a Beatle refusing to kneel before the Queen of England.

"Let's just talk about your business" would have been similarly shocking. Senior leaders at IBM in the early '90s *couldn't* just talk about their businesses because they didn't know their businesses. They worked through a thick cloud of assistants and intermediaries who preprocessed their information for them. Most decisions in the company at that time were actually made by a small group of folks called the "Management Committee," which essentially absolved executives from the decision-making responsibilities of their roles.[45] Asking to have a conversation about business performance in such an environment was nothing less than rubbing their lack of competence in their faces. Gerstner valued humility, hands-on leadership, and frank communication. The entrenched IBM culture and its sclerotic leadership simply was incapable of performing in the way Gerstner needed them to.

Quoth Gerstner:

"Until I came to IBM, I probably would have told you that culture was just one among several important elements in any organization's makeup and success—along with vision, strategy, marketing, financials, and the like. I came to see, in my time at IBM, that culture isn't just one aspect of the game; it is the game. In the end, an organization is nothing more than the collective capacity of its people to create value."[46]

Gerstner didn't need an eloquent speech to kick off a revolution. He just needed to flip a switch.

We can do the same.

Every culture has its taboos, its shibboleths, that which cannot be done, or said, or that which cannot be criticized. The most effective way to communicate that this is Day One of the new company is to boldly violate one of these taboos.

I was leading a very important project concerning the complete redesign of a supply-chain company's network strategy. Similar efforts had failed several times before, often due to lack of leadership engagement or competing agendas. When I accepted the responsibility for this effort, I vowed that we would do things differently than we had in the past, emphasizing the principles of collaboration, innovation, and transparency. The company at this time had what the new CEO referred to (publicly!) as "a passive-aggressive culture"; those three values could not have been more at odds with the prevailing culture.

The first meeting with senior leadership and the project team was therefore going to be my equivalent to the Gerstner "Foils Foiled" meeting. Unfortunately, I had precisely none of Gerstner's positional authority; I was just a guy running a big project.

For any meetings involving the leadership team, the normal setup was for them to sit in a line of chairs facing the audience, parallel to the presenter. For presentations with lots of slides to read, they would be in the front row facing the presenter.

I put a table at the front and sat the leadership team around it, with the rest of the team sitting in chairs set up theater-style.

This immediately made people nervous.

I came back into the room at one point to see that it had been rearranged. I put it back the way I had it.

I received a number of comments, mostly negative, regarding the planned layout. No one could articulate why it was bad; they just *knew* it was bad.

Then my second edict hit. No laptops. No phones. For the 60 minutes we were together, we would be discussing this topic. Together. Indeed, I sat most of the team theater-style so that they couldn't work on their laptops. I wanted their full focus to be on the task at hand.

I sat the leadership team the way I did to silently communicate the culture change we needed:

1. **This was a collaboration.** Sitting at a table together meant that we were working together. Having the leadership team at the only table together placed the priority on the leadership team collaborating—that is, this being a truly cross-functional effort.
2. **There would be transparency.** The team was facing the leadership team as they worked. No one was focused on anything else at the moment except for this effort.
3. **There would be innovation.** This was a new way to present information and have a discussion in a large meeting setting. We would not be doing what we had done in the past. We needed to change.

To my delight, one representative of the old guard refused to comply, commandeered a small table, and sat in the back of the room with her laptop and her phone. I completely ignored her, allowing her to stand in as a silent example of the dysfunction of the past. If I had asked her to do something to help me underscore the difference between the ossified culture that was strangling our company and the way in which we needed to operate in order to save it, she would never have done so. She did us a tremendous service that day, nonetheless, by modeling the bad habits representative of the obsolete culture.

We had PowerPoint slides for the meeting, but most of it was interactive. My primary objective beyond disturbing the status quo was to ensure that the representatives from each area on our core and extended teams had the full proxy of the leaders at the table and could make decisions on their behalf. Mission accomplished. With frequent interaction from the team members, we also managed to erode the hierarchy a bit, and based on comments after the meeting, the team felt excited and empowered. A good start—but only a start. By daring to violate some taboos, we gained needed momentum.

Napoleon Bonaparte did the same when he took the crown from the Pope's hands and crowned himself Emperor of the French, a new kind of monarch for a new kind of France. Alexander the Great did it when adopting Persian dress, taking a Persian wife, and allowing his Persian subjects to abase themselves before him, scandalizing his Macedonian veterans but sending the message that under Alexander's reign all peoples would be one. General Ulysses S. Grant showed up to accept General Robert E. Lee's surrender in muddy boots and his everyday uniform, despite the momentous occasion, making it clear that Grant was a republican soldier and not a high-born gentleman. Singer Bono from the band U2 climbed over barriers at the Live Aid event to embrace and dance with ordinary fans, horrifying security but delighting people all over the world and reinforcing that this was no ordinary rock concert. The buttoned-down world of test cricket was rocked when Douglas Jardine, English team captain, unveiled the "Bodyline" strategy of fast bowling at the legs of batsmen against the Australians in 1932, shaking up a sport which had hitherto prided itself on gentlemanly play. It takes great leaders to do such small things.

Once the initial shock wave has dissipated, it must be followed up with tangible actions and small wins, lest one turn out not to be a great leader so much as a run-of-the-mill iconoclast. A company in crisis being a target-rich environment, the main trouble may be figuring out where to begin. Look for the following opportunities to either stop, start, or improve how we do things:

- Biggest gap between current and desired culture
- Things customers hate most about the company
- Restoring past practices employees loved but company eliminated
- Practices despised by employees
- Worst examples of leadership dysfunction
- Bureaucratic processes
- Sources of friction between teams
- Obstacles to doing the right thing
- People who have demonstrated poor integrity
- Poorly performing teams
- Individuals who are already exemplars of the new culture

It's highly possible (if not very likely) that you may find yourself confronted with too many examples and need some way to sort them based on magnitude of benefit. The model below offers a quick-and-dirty way of doing this:

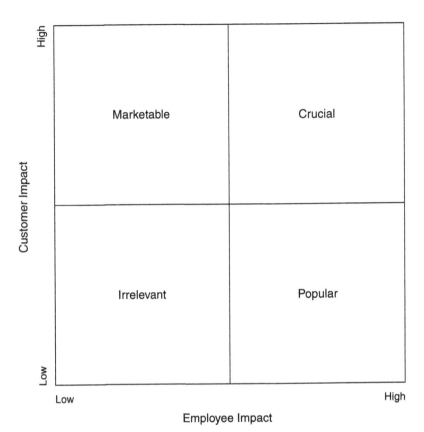

FIGURE 32. Cultural opportunity assessment model

- **Irrelevant.** Don't waste any time thinking about or acting upon such things at this stage. It will only divert resources.
- **Popular.** Especially early on, it may be wise to do some internal things to build morale and buy-in. A little bit goes a long way.
- **Marketable.** A company in crisis needs to shore up revenue streams almost prior to any other consideration. If you can do something to delight or merely retain a customer, do it. The customer should feel the culture change even before the teammates on the floor, if only because senior leadership demonstrates a renewed commitment to actually listening to the customer.
- **Crucial.** Anywhere you see an opportunity which will make customers and employees happy, move heaven and earth to realize it.

Once the opportunities are selected, they should be aggressively pursued and the results tracked and reported. As work progresses, there will naturally arise occasions where behaviors associated with the emerging culture can be observed and reinforced, while those associated with the old culture can be discouraged. By the end of these first projects, we should therefore have tangible positive results banked and dozens of employees who now have practical experience with how the new culture operates.

Step Four: Assimilate into the New Culture

The first projects undertaken in accordance with a cultural transformation are fine, but the depth and breadth of the effort must swiftly increase if the entire company is to evolve. Those first actions are merely the springboard to driving adoption of the new culture across the entire enterprise. In order to accomplish this much larger objective, we will need to repeat the following process:

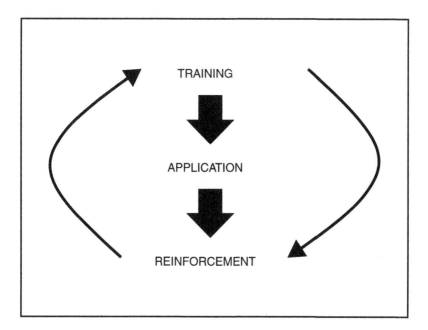

FIGURE 33. Cultural assimilation process

This simple model is the basis for utterly transforming companies.

- **Training.** If we want people to behave differently, we first have to teach them how we want them to behave. A colleague of mine once shared with us an old New England Patriots football playbook. Readers will recall that the Patriots have been the most successful franchise in the National Football League over the past two decades.[47] The first page of the playbook was devoted to detailed instructions as to how to form a huddle, the between-plays formation offensive players get into in order to receive the play call from the quarterback. The reason that a professional football team comprised of players who had been huddling up for some 20 years at this point was simple: If you cannot form a proper huddle, you will not always know which play is being run; and if you don't know which play is being run, you cannot do your job on that play. If we want our company's players to be able to do the job they need to do, we need to teach them at the most basic level what our expectations are, even when it seems a bit silly to have to teach seasoned professionals such behaviors.
- **Application.** Training isn't much good without plenty of practice and application. The Patriots don't simply quiz players on how to huddle then forget about it. They huddle up on every offensive play, getting thousands of repetitions in by the time the season officially starts and ensuring that no matter how the players may have huddled previously, they were now doing it the Patriot Way. We must do the same with regard to company culture. It is not sufficient for supervisors to sit through a lecture on employee empowerment. They must leave the meeting and put the principle into practice by allowing their teams to make decisions on their own that the supervisor previously made.
- **Reinforcement.** Humans are creatures of habit. If we are to overcome these habits, we must constantly reinforce those behaviors that comprise the new culture and suppress those which are unique to the old. To the Patriots, this means that whenever someone deviates from proper huddling, they will receive prompt correction, most likely by the quarterback, but certainly by a coach. Every play is filmed so there is nowhere for an offender to hide. Relentless mutual accountability ensures that the culture is maintained. If we are driving employee empowerment, we must praise those supervisors who are allowing employees to make appropriate decisions at their level and correct those who are not. Normally we praise in public and punish in private, but in the case of

cultural transformations, it may be necessary to make an example of someone publicly, particularly in the early going of the effort. It is more important to drive the right behavior than to protect anyone's ego. Not everyone will make the transition to the new culture.[48]

The curved arrows on the diagram are there to indicate that this is a repetitive process, not a "one-and-done." Transformation efforts often kick off with a big-bang training session, and once those few hours are done, no one gets additional training over the life of the project. This is the wrong way to go about fundamental change. I will never forget the experience I had at Bank of America when new leadership of our quality team commissioned a large, complicated illustration (something to do with river rapids) that looked like a board game designed by someone at *MAD Magazine*.[49] They brought us in for a half-day training session on this culture change, which basically involved greater centralization of Six Sigma projects. As that began to manifest, one of my Master Black Belt colleagues leaned over to me and whispered, "So after spending all this time building relationships with our business partners and becoming trusted advisers, they want us to stop helping our business partners and focus instead on stuff the business doesn't care about?" I nodded. "Well," she said, "time to go get a job in the business." She was exactly right. Once business partners had the chance to talk to one another and compare notes about this new direction, the new leaders were sacked, and we went back to the previous mode of operations. It is simply not enough to present the training material and assume all will be well.

Application and reinforcement must be continuous as well. Where Six Sigma has foundered, it has done so because of insufficient follow-up on Green Belt certifications. What I mean by this is that there is usually a big push at the outset of a Six Sigma implementation to train a bunch of folks and get them going on their Green Belt projects. Then there's a big wave of certifications. And after that, nothing. Sure, a relative handful of business leaders will really take to the methodology and go on to pursue Black Belt and even Master Black Belt certification. But the vast majority will simply pack up their binders and stick them on the shelf. After a short while the project activity will abate, and people will go back to whatever they were doing before, leading a number to write articles on LinkedIn about how "Six Sigma doesn't work."

The best way to ensure that training, application, and reinforcement are continuous is by putting in place metrics and using them to drive accountability, aided by embedding the new culture into the recognition and performance management processes. We will discuss these topics later in the context of sustaining the new culture.

This process should be sufficient to get most employees up and running in the new culture, but what of the holdouts? What do we do about those teams and individuals who continue to resist transitioning to the new and better way of doing things?

This is a two-part problem. First, we must smoke out resistance. After the success of our shock-and-awe campaign, and this active pursuit to get everyone in the company practicing the new way of doing things, it should be expected that opponents of the new culture have gone underground. What once was aggressive resistance has now become passive-aggressive. If we have done a reasonable job in defining and tracking metrics indicative of the level of adoption of the culture, we may well spot those teams that are underperforming. If not, we may have a sufficient network of allies now willing to turn informant. Failing that, we can spend more time with those of suspect allegiance to the new way of doing things and will surely get a feel for the true commitment level over time. Once we know where the resistance is, we can either retrain, reassign, or terminate the employment of the recalcitrant employees.

There will no doubt come a time during this phase where a moment of truth will arrive. Most likely this will come in the form of some minor setback to overall progress which gives heart to opponents of the change and causes everyone else to wonder, if only for an instant, whether or not this is all going to work out. There will be a strong temptation to go back to the old ways just until this minor crisis has passed. In our employee-empowerment example, this crisis might arise when an employee makes a bad decision (after all, we all know that supervisors *never* made a bad decision in the good ol' days). The easy answer would be to remove decision-making authority from the lower-level employee on at least a temporary basis. The right answer would be to understand what information the employee had available to then, why the decision was the wrong one to make, and hold the employee accountable for their part in the decision. After all, accountability without empowerment is tyranny; empowerment without accountability is anarchy. We don't want either.

Step Five: Grow the New Culture

It may seem at this point that the objectives of the transformation have been met, but this would be a very dangerous presumption. It is rather like transplanting a tree to new soil. It may appear stout and hearty, but the first contrary wind will topple it. We must protect our new culture from the inevitable storms until its roots have sunk deeply enough into the company that it becomes unmovable.

In order to prepare for long-term sustainability of the culture, we must accomplish the following tasks:

- Identify those who will be guardians of the new culture and train them in how to nurture it.
- Neutralize remaining opposition to the new culture.
- Embed new cultural norms deeply into all company processes and purge vestiges of the old culture from them.
- Weight performance review, hiring, bonuses, and employee growth in favor of new cultural behaviors.

The point of this step is to ensure that there will be no going back to the old culture and all of the problems it spawned. It is the point of no return. In Jewish weddings, at the moment when a couple is pronounced man and wife, a wedding glass is placed on the ground and stamped by the groom, symbolizing the finality of the marital bond so created. For this reason, at one company I worked for we used to refer to the importance of sunsetting old information technology systems as "breaking glass." American naval captain John Paul Jones reached a similar moment in a battle against the British Royal Navy during the Revolutionary War. His much smaller vessel, *Bonhomme Richard*, outgunned, overmatched, foundering, and with the wind dying, rammed *Serapis*. The American sailors had no choice but to fight or die at that point; they triumphed, and Jones became a legend ("I have not yet begun to fight!" he was said to have said, securing his place in military history).[50]

It is therefore necessary in the aftermath of the triumph of the new culture to completely dismantle the old. If decisions had to previously be made by a committee, get rid of the committee. If we used a certain type of performance review system prior to the new culture, junk it and implement a new one. If we gave out the Marine Drill Instructor Award for Loudest Yelling at Employees before, melt down the trophies. Knock down walls. Repaint. Throw away pictures on the walls. Have a big bonfire and purge the company forever of the burdens of the past. If it reeks of the Bad Old Days, it stinks.

Purging the nonphysical may be even more important. If there were words and phrases (memes, really) associated with the previous culture, they must be uprooted. At Bank of America, the practice of typing running commentary on what people were saying in a meeting using the messaging program Sametime was referred to as "the Sametime undercurrent," a practice an enterprising executive on the technology team sought to stamp out utterly. "Voluntold" was the Air Force practice of couching direct orders in requests for volunteers. Punctuality was enforced with: "If you aren't 15 minutes early, you're 15 minutes late." My beloved Oakland Raiders coined the phrase, "If you ain't cheatin', you ain't tryin.'" Language is a vehicle for culture; as the culture changes, so must the language. When one company I worked for brought in external consultants to help with our transformation, they used a meme wherein a horizontal line was drawn on a whiteboard. Everything below the line was negative and horrible; everything above was positive and wonderful. They used "above the line" and "below the line" to promote the behavior they wanted and condemn the behavior they didn't want. Of course, the reactionaries responded with a meme of their own: "If you aren't below the line around here, you aren't paying attention."

The last item on the To Do List for growing your culture is to celebrate your victories. The aforementioned bonfire can be a part of this celebration, inviting volunteers (not the "voluntold," please)[51] to enjoy the catharsis of unburdening themselves of the past by tossing it on the pyre. A review of the progress to date is certainly warranted, as is a reminder of just how bad things were at the beginning of the transformation. Testimonials from customers and employees are helpful. Saying goodbye to the transformation team and hello to the newly appointed guardians of the culture would be a great idea and a classy touch to boot. Having some physical sign of the permanency of the transformation would be terrific; after all, the victors of every war like to erect monuments. Above all, the event should be an expression of gratitude toward all those who beat the odds and successfully transformed the company's culture and thereby ensured the continued survival of the firm.

Presuming the company manages to sustain the new culture, that is.

ELEVEN

Sustaining Your Culture

"Growing a culture requires a good storyteller. Changing a culture requires a persuasive editor."

—RYAN LILLY

Whether your company's culture has changed through conformation, reformation, or transformation, we are now at the point in its development where the editor hands the pen to the storyteller. Every new creation must have its founding myth. The Latin poet Virgil linked that of Rome to the fall of Troy, the greatest myth of the ancient world.[52] GE harkens back to Thomas Edison's laboratory. At Bank of America, the founding myth involved the great earthquake and fire of 1906 in San Francisco and a stalwart banker making loans to neighbors in the rubble so they could rebuild the city. Amazonians tell and retell the story of Jeff Bezos's founding of the company in his garage, a classic tale of the lone visionary fighting for a dream no one else could comprehend at the time. How many of these legends have we been taught about how our countries came to be? How closely do they adhere to reality?

If we want our companies and their new cultures to thrive, we need to harness the power of mythmaking to inspire people long after those of us who made this change happen are gone. Earlier, we discussed how the meme is the common currency of the culture. We are going to mint some new money capable of carrying our values far into the future.

Our tale is going to be modeled on "The Hero's Journey" defined by Joseph Campbell.[53] Since this is going to be a very short story rather than an epic poem, we're going to hit the major beats but not necessarily each and every one that Campbell defines.

Here is the structure of the monomyth, as Campbell laid it out:

Part	Stage	Description
Call to Adventure	The Ordinary World	The hero sets out from the mundane world.
	The Call to Adventure	Something causes him to want to leave.
	Refusal	Something makes him want to stay.
Supreme Ordeal/ Initiation	Mentor Helper	Someone appears to help him on his journey.
	Crossing the Threshold	The point of no return is reached.
	Test/Allies/Enemies	Obstacles and foes waylay the hero.
Unification/ Transformation	Approach	A major challenge comes into view.
	Ordeal	The hero suffers in some fashion.
	Reward	After prevailing, the hero receives a boon.
Road Back/ Hero's Return	Road Back	On the way back home, more obstacles are encountered.
	Atonement	The hero reflects on what he has learned from his journey.
	Return	Normality is restored.

FIGURE 34. Founding myth structure

First, we must choose our hero. Humility being essential, and sustainability of the legend requiring that the hero be "one of us," choose someone from the company rather than an outsider or yourself. Your pick should be someone who was essential to the overall effort and typifies the values of the new culture. Polarizing figures should be avoided wherever possible. Once chosen, we'll apply the Hero's Journey story structure as follows:

- **The Ordinary World.** Describe what the company was like before the transformation began. Emphasize the negative. Alternatively, invoke a past golden age of the company; then describe how it lost its way.
- **The Call to Adventure.** Relate how our hero first became aware of the need for the company's culture to change.

- **Refusal.** What made it so difficult for the hero to embrace that need for change? What resistance did she face? What fears did she have?
- **Mentor Helper.** Describe how others came to help bring about the transformation. How did they win our hero's trust?
- **Crossing the Threshold.** What was the turning point where the hero committed to the change and bringing it about?
- **Tests/Allies/Enemies.** What initial challenges did our hero have to overcome?
- **Approach.** What was the biggest challenge she faced?
- **Ordeal.** How did the hero overcome this challenge?
- **Reward.** How did the hero and the company benefit from this triumph?
- **Road Back.** What additional problems had to be resolved to make the new culture the new normal?
- **Atonement.** What did the hero learn from this?
- **Return.** Describe the better world the hero has brought about and the hopes for the future that come with it.

Throughout this chapter we've described a situation where a portion of the culture change involved increasing employee empowerment. Let's use that as a basis for an example:

The story above is certainly not worthy of Tolstoy (although it may feel nearly as long as *War and Peace*), but Dani's tale fits the bill for describing the journey the company has been on in a way that resonates with people. There will always be a Dani in any cultural transformation if you only take the time to look for her.

Once we have our founding myth, we need to tell it again and again. Put it on the company website. Create a "Dani Award for Employee Empowerment." Add Dani to our corporate lexicon: "I took over my team and realized I needed to Dani things up—now they love their work!" Get the marketing team to create a Dani brand. Make an acronym out of her name: "Decisions Are Not Inventory." Write songs. Make videos. Create video games. Whatever it takes to tell the heroic story of our culture warrior and what she did, do it.

Metrics

"Tell me how you're measured, I'll tell you how you'll behave" is an old saw in quality circles.[54] Metrics drive behavior. If we measure the right metrics and

Part	Stage	Description
Call to Adventure	The Ordinary World	Dani Montana ran the customer service call center for the company. When she first started with us 25 years ago, it was wonderful: she loved working with our customers and could solve problems quickly and completely. Over time, though, customer service came to be more and more scripted. Her team required her approval for 86% of all issues. Dani had to request approval herself for 34%. Customers grew more and more unhappy, as these approvals took a long time.
	The Call to Adventure	The company started to lose major accounts. Dani knew several of the key people on these accounts personally and wanted to reach out to them to understand their pain and urge them to stay.
	Refusal	Unfortunately, the company had just issued a new rule preventing customer service from getting engaged with the customer relationship beyond simply resolving the problems the customer identified. It made no sense to Dani, but it was company policy.
Supreme Ordeal/ Initiation	Mentor Helper	Then, the Transformation Team was formed. At first Dani thought it would just result in being micromanaged by outsiders, but when she saw how committed the team was to empowering teammates, she decided to help in any way she could.
	Crossing the Threshold	That is when a major client reached out to her and told her that they were so unhappy with the issues and poor customer service that they were going to bid out the contract. "What happened to you guys, Dani? You used to be the best!" Dani decided to do something. She arranged to meet the client for lunch, told them that big changes were coming and that she expected soon to be able to directly help resolve the client's issues. The customer gave the company another 90 days to do something.
	Test/Allies/ Enemies	The sales rep for that customer caught wind of the meeting Dani had and complained to his boss and her boss. "You don't have the authority to promise that customer a thing! Follow your script!" he said. Dani was put on a performance plan.
Unification/ Transformation	Approach	The Transformation Team scheduled a series of reviews with customers to understand their concerns. The customer told them about Dani and expressed disappointment that they were not seeing any real progress yet.

(continued)

Part	Stage	Description
	Ordeal	Dani was called in by the Transformation Team to explain the situation. Didn't she understand that she needed to empower her team to support the client better? Dani struggled to compose herself, then explained to the audience that she was being prevented from empowering her team by two executives and a counterproductive policy. Her boss grew angry and defensive, claiming that she didn't have the experience to manage so large a client and needed to stick to her job or find another. The Chief Transformation Officer listened quietly, then asked, "What is her job?" Her boss answered, "To solve customer problems." "Then why aren't you letting her do it?"
	Reward	Dani was asked to rewrite the policy in question in a way more consistent with the new culture. She was also given responsibility for managing the relationship with the client in question until normalcy could be restored. The Chief Transformation Officer requested her performance plan be removed.
Road Back/ Hero's Return	Road Back	Dani presented her ideas in a number of forums and fought for their adoption. She managed to demonstrate such progress with the client that she received their award for Supplier of the Year on behalf of the company. The relationship with her boss was still sour, and he was reassigned.
	Atonement	Dani realized how important it was to have power along with accountability. She also realized her team needed that same flexibility. She eliminated 95% of the items requiring her approval, pushing them down to her team. She invested in training them so they could make good decisions, and worked with other teams to make sure they had all the relevant information at their disposal. In the end, the escalation rate dropped to less than 5%.
	Return	Dani's world is a much happier one today. Customers are very well taken care of, with over 90% of their problems being resolved in 10 minutes or less. Turnover in her area has dropped by 60%. Moreover, she and her team know that the company places great faith in them and trusts them to take great care of the customer. "We lost our way for a little while and thought that tighter control of approvals would keep bad things from happening. We didn't realize that we were really making sure that bad things did happen, especially by not trusting our teammates to do their jobs. Now we rely on everyone to do their best, always. We're a team again!"

FIGURE 35. Founding myth example

respond in rational ways to their performance, we can sustain the right behavior over the long term.

We must measure our culture.

In Chapter 5, we covered cultural assessment and provided some useful tools for performing one. We should certainly refresh that assessment periodically and determine whether we have any yawning gaps between our culture as communicated, understood, and lived by our employees. We should then take action to close these gaps.

If we are truly living our culture, however, we shouldn't need to rely on a special assessment in order to know how we're living up to our ideals. These metrics should be fully integrated into our regular reporting routines. In our empowerment example, it would be quite useful to provide some way of tracking how decentralized decision-making is within the organization between surveys. As a Lean practitioner, I'm particularly fond of time-based metrics: a running stopwatch doesn't lie. We could get a decent gauge of how bureaucratic we are simply by defining important business processes and timing how long it takes to get a decision. The retail industry is fond of "secret shopper" data collection techniques whereby an employee or consultant pretends to be a customer in order to get direct indications of customer experience. This approach could be used to test whether frontline, customer-facing employees are being allowed to resolve issues at their level. If you have a particularly strong devotion to business process management and have invested in fully documenting processes and workflows, you may be able to pull some data directly regarding who made key decisions and craft an indicator based on the organizational level of that decision-maker. With a little creativity and a bit of curiosity, you can craft a very useful scorecard pointing toward trends in the health of your company's culture.

Operating Routines

Metrics are only as good as they are monitored and drive business decisions. If no one looks or takes action based on your cultural health scorecard, all it will have recorded is the demise of the culture. Scorecards must be reviewed, discussed, and addressed by business leaders. Given that the culture is the means by which the company delivers value, this information is of great importance to all levels of the organization. Just as many companies have incorporated safety and quality portions of every meeting, cultural discussion ought to take pride of place as safety and quality are products of the culture.

Include culture in the agenda of the following meetings:

- Shift standups
- Project reviews
- Performance reviews
- Production
- Town halls
- All hands
- Leadership
- Board
- Road shows
- Budget reviews

The following should be considered for routine discussion of culture in these operating routines:

- **Values.** Choose a particular value, read its definition, and share what it means to you.
- **Behaviors.** Discuss what behaviors are associated with particular values.
- **Heroes.** Recognize someone within the organization for epitomizing the values of the culture and share their story.
- **Case studies.** Listen to audio or watch a video showing teammates interacting with other teammates or customers. Assess how well the interaction aligned with the culture and make suggestions for improvement.
- **Feedback.** Ask how the team feels about how the culture is being lived.
- **Suggestions.** Ask how the culture can be improved and lived more deeply.

Even if the amount of time set aside within a given meeting is trivial, the constant repetition underscores the primary importance of the culture. Moreover, it reinforces the notion that while leadership may define culture, culture is owned by every employee. It lives.

Performance Management

Culture is *everything*.

There is simply no such thing as a great company with a lousy culture; as soon as the culture slips, the company's performance slides. We've discussed many examples underlining this reality; I'll provide one more to drive the point home. It is a story near and dear to my heart as a lifetime fan of comic books.

From 1961 to 1991, Marvel Comics was renowned as "The House of Ideas." Under the guiding hand of Stan "The Man" Lee, Marvel grew from an also-ran cranking out a handful of poorly read monster and romance comics each month to dominate the industry by creating a unique company culture which attracted older fans (comics had previously targeted the prepubescent market) and birthed what we now call "nerd culture." In addition to creating more sophisticated and emotionally resonant stories ("The World Outside Your Door") than the competition, Stan created a fictional "Marvel Bullpen," which made it sound as though the company was just one big happy (and comically dysfunctional) team having the time of their lives making great comics. This unique culture came to be referred to as "The Marvel Method," an innovative way to approach comics where artists would discuss the general plot with Lee and draw the book, and Lee would then add the captions and word balloons to finish the story. It shifted power from the editor and scripter to the artist, who was also encouraged to draw the most action-oriented stories possible.

By 1991, Lee had turned over the editor-in-chief reins and decamped to Hollywood to follow his dream of seeing the heroes he'd created with the most talented artists in the industry on the silver screen. The comic book boom was on, and speculators started invading the hobby, viewing comics as potentially lucrative, collectible investments. Writers and artists commanded larger salaries, exclusive contracts, royalties, and rock-star levels of celebrity that had never been seen before. The number of comics available ballooned, publishers proliferated, and specialty shops replaced the drugstore comics racks as customers skewed older.

The books themselves became much more violent, dark, and risqué; I could never have bought these comics when I started collecting as a ten-year-old. They garnered real respect in the artistic community as a legitimate and worthwhile medium. The prices skyrocketed, as did the quality of the paper and ink of which they were made.

Along the way, Marvel had lost its heart.

No longer committed to telling great stories, Marvel (and most of its competition) began to indulge in gimmicks designed to milk customers a little more: variant covers, restarting long-running series with new #1 issues to draw in the speculators, killing key characters, crossover events requiring collectors to buy dozens of books they didn't like in order to complete the story, flooding the racks with new titles (with worse and worse art; pencillers can only produce so many pages a month). They'd even fired editor-in-chief Jim Shooter, the man who, post-Stan, had driven Marvel to dominance within the industry, replacing him with a series of former editors who never seemed to have a coherent publishing strategy.

Sales declined, costs remained high, creators left to become competitors, and Marvel went bankrupt in 1996. Legal battles ensued, and this might have been the inglorious end of the Marvel story had Toy Biz CEO Avi Arad not convinced Hollywood (and Merrill Lynch) to make a big bet on the timeless appeal of those well-nigh-unrecognizable heroes Stan Lee and his collaborators had dreamed up in the early '60s.

The success of the Marvel Cinematic Universe and related toys refilled Marvel's coffers and created renewed interest in the comics. A new generation of creators who had grown up on Stan Lee's comics took the helm of the comics side of the business, got back to the business of telling great stories in much the way Stan had, and brought the company's culture back from the dead.[55]

As much as I wish that the company had managed to completely turn back time, what it did do in the earliest years of the twenty-first century was sufficient to turn things around, with the comic stories in effect now seen as storyboards for a burgeoning slate of blockbuster films and licensed properties. This would simply have been impossible given the awfulness of the culture in the mid-'90s and the counterproductive behavior this drove.

So, if culture is everything, why do so many businesses act as though employees embracing their culture is a "nice to have" item? Why do we continually prize output metric performance ("making your number") over demonstrating behavior that aligns with the culture?

Several years ago, an employee who was leaving the company indicated in an e-mail to me that her team was gaming the performance management system and told me how they were doing it. This disturbed me greatly, not least because every morning I walked through the lobby where our values were emblazoned in bronze over the entryways and no fewer than three of these spoke to honor and integrity. Moreover, since the performance management system was tied to salary increases, promotions, and bonuses, these teammates were effectively stealing from the company. Even worse, I knew the executive over that area well, considered him a friend, and when I notified him of this problem, he was very dismissive of my concern, leaving the distinct impression that he already knew about it and may even have sanctioned it.

I escalated the issue to the vice president of that area, a former naval officer. He immediately put his entire team on notice that that practice ceased that day, and anyone who did something similar would be run out of the company. He clearly believed that cultural values like integrity were more important than making your number; indeed, making your number didn't even factor into the calculation when it came to dealing with cheaters and liars.

Those are rare birds indeed in my experience. Too many leaders are simply willing to compromise, even if they realize that it will never pay off in the long run.

For our cultures and our companies to thrive, however, it is absolutely essential that we manage performance on a "culture first" basis. There's not much to talk about regarding the numbers in a performance review; you've either made them or you didn't, a fact known well in advance of the discussion. What really matters is how you conduct yourself and whether or not you help the team succeed and are a good ambassador for the company.

In most performance management systems, how an employee does his work is on the face of it given equal footing with what they have done. In reality, however, top performers in terms of output will be given top marks in the "soft skills" as well, a necessity for promotion. This is true even if the person is a narcissist or a psychopath—and perhaps truer if they are. Senior executives in many cases will put up with someone who is absolutely horrible to deal with just as long as the numbers look good.

Sustaining a culture that works will therefore require a small leap of faith. If you believe as I do that culture is everything, if you believe that culture eats strategy for breakfast, if you believe that culture drives excellent performance and not vice versa, then you must put culture first. Rack-and-stack your organization based on cultural fit. Spend 75% of your coaching and assessment time on improving cultural alignment. Get used to having open and frank discussions about values and behaviors, constantly probing to understand whether or not the other person is committed or merely going through the motions. Give your bonuses out primarily on the basis of who lives the culture. Here's the big one: put someone on a performance plan who is crushing their numbers but not living the culture. If you have the guts to do that, you'll be a legend to your people.

If you're truly committed, you'll take the next step of asking your direct reports for their feedback regarding how well you're living the culture. Nothing could inspire your team more than humbling yourself before them by admitting you have work to do on one or more of the values or behaviors required of your culture. Walk that talk!

Hiring and Firing

There is no better way to reinforce commitment to your culture than in hiring and firing on the basis of culture fit. Too much of the interview process is spent understanding a candidate's background, which is never fully relevant. As they say in the small print in advertising, past performance does not guarantee future performance. Our increasingly technocratic society augments this error with pop quizzes and long checklists of skills. Even were this approach fully accurate and predictive, it still wouldn't matter because job descriptions are terribly written, and most teammates will hold numerous roles during their tenure at a company.

Far better to focus on culture fit. If someone has poor SQL coding skills, they can master it given a few months and some training. If they cannot work with people, you've got bigger problems, as business is a team sport. I hire for attitude, not certitude. Curiosity, humility, commitment, integrity, and a positive outlook lifts the performance of an entire team in a way that one prima donna who's terrific at what they do simply can't, being just one person.

Addition by subtraction works out in similar fashion. I would rather see a high-performing *enfant terrible* walk than lose the otherwise-average heart and soul of the team. I'm not sentimental; the team's performance is worse with the show pony than it is with the workhorse. An employee who is constantly working against the grain of your culture is unlikely to work out in the long run anyway, like a vegetarian hunter. Replacing a nonbeliever with a true believer can turn around the dynamics on your team overnight.

Process Design

If our company culture is what enables us to do what we must do, it stands to reason that everything we do should reflect our cultural values in some way. I recently had an issue with Amazon.com, a company that prides itself on customer service. I'd ordered some nice patio furniture. Soon after ordering, the freight carrier called me to ask if I would be willing to receive it a couple of days early, a request to which I agreed. I arranged to work from home that day so I could help my wife unpack the furniture. The delivery window came and went. An hour later, the carrier called me to say that they had not received the delivery at their hub (a fact I knew from experience they had surely known the night before) and seeking a delivery window the next day. I had to go into the office but planned to be home by the time the delivery arrived. Of course, the window came and went again, and I called the carrier, who told me the driver had left late, was an hour away, and I was his third stop. I let the carrier have it and told them I would call Amazon. They were unperturbed.

To my surprise, I had to escalate to a customer service supervisor at Amazon, as the first associate wouldn't help me beyond giving me a $75 gift card, which was fine but didn't resolve my problem. I wound up having to lecture the supervisor on Amazon's culture and threaten to cancel my Prime membership (which I've had since it was first offered). She mainly just mirrored my verbiage and offered to call the carrier. She called me back to say that the carrier was coming straight to my house and I'd been bumped to first priority in the truck (there were two other deliveries on that truck). When the carrier showed up, late again, my wife noticed the truck was completely empty once our delivery was off of it. They had simply lied. I notified Amazon and was assured they would file some sort of complaint with the carrier (which of course I never saw).

All this episode really accomplished was to confirm that Amazon.com really doesn't care about putting the customer first. I had moved my schedule around to accommodate their freight carrier, only to get the runaround and the added insult of being lied to. I had previously been confident that Amazon would move heaven and earth to get my order to me on time, particularly after the first botched delivery. Instead, they acted as though it were completely out of their hands and, moreover, that they had no interest in it. This, from a company which revolutionized customer experience in the Internet Age! I will simply never order another item from them that requires a freight carrier.

The culprit was most likely process design.

Amazon began by handling its own fulfillment in partnership with UPS, almost exclusively on a small parcel basis. The company retained firm control over the entire process and insisted on the best customer experience possible. As the company grew and its supply chain grew ever more complicated, it began to leverage third-party logistics partners who neither shared their commitment to customers nor had the operational skill to ensure deliveries went smoothly. If Amazon ever closely monitored these third parties, they stopped doing so at some point, and in so doing compromised the supreme value in their culture. They failed to properly design their processes to maximize customer experience and therefore lost their edge.

Amazon is a great company. If it can happen to them, it can happen to any of us.

The best way to avoid this fate is to design our processes in ways that align with our values. If we're a Lean culture, our processes should be streamlined and waste-free. Websites should be clean and intuitive. Information, goods, and services should be presented to customers on demand and not before. If we're a Six Sigma culture, you had better believe everything we do needs to be error-free; those spelling errors on the homepage are going to be the source of much online mockery otherwise. If we claim to innovate, but do what everyone else in our industry does, we'll look quite foolish.

We can uncover processes that do not align with our ideals simply by walking through them and giving a grade for each value, then ensure our next redesign emphasizes fixes to the lowest-scoring values. A similar cultural alignment matrix could be used in our process design and process improvement project deliverables, ensuring that anytime we work on a process, we leave behind an engine for reinforcing who we are and what we want to be.

We can build cultural alignment as a criterion within our audits, generating findings wherever we uncover practices that do not conform with our culture. This can be an effective way of keeping sprawling operations standardized and could even extend up the supply chain, ensuring seamless customer experience of the sort quite unlike what I experienced in my patio furniture delivery anecdote.

Customers and regulators will hold your company accountable for the performance of every link in your supply chain; it would be very wise to source based on cultural compatibility.

Project Management

Much of the work done by process improvement professionals is organized along project lines, which implies that building a culture congruent with maximizing continuous improvement requires living out that culture within our projects.

The following tips will help bring culture and project management into closer alignment:

- **Project selection.** Selection process should feature criteria that sustain or improve the culture as communicated, understood, and lived. Improving the culture should be a sufficient reason to charter a project.
- **Project roles.** We should be careful to ensure that senior roles on the project are filled with regard to who lives our culture best, for similar reasons to those covered in the performance management section above.
- **Project timelines.** Time must be included once the improvement plan is crafted to allow for assessment for cultural alignment. This will ensure that any improvements implemented will be consistent with the company's culture. There are also often process changes which could be made which are inconsistent with the culture; these should be eliminated.
- **Project tollgates.** Tollgate questions should include probing for cultural alignment and impact, with an eye toward preventing unintended consequences. Keeping projects aligned with our culture should be a top priority of leaders determining the future course of these initiatives.
- **Control plans.** Ensure that there are elements within the plan to make certain that alignment with the culture is maintained. Cultural alignment should be treated as a critical-to-quality feature of the project.
- **Communication plans.** These must be consistent with the culture. If your culture places a high value on customer experience, for example, you won't want to surprise online customers with changes or make them dig through your tech support site to read release notes.

Training

A culture widely lived is one that trains without trainers or, depending upon how you look at it, perhaps it trains with a mighty host of trainers. Newcomers adapt to such cultures in much the way foreign-language students do when traveling in the countries where their subject is the prevailing tongue.

Most companies will require some sort of cultural training, especially for new hires. Even the longest-tenured personnel benefit from a refresher course on the finer points of the culture along with an invitation to meditate more deeply on its values and behaviors and a recommitment to its principles. The following suggestions regarding culture training should prove useful:

- **Train all new hires.** Do not run the risk of new teammates picking up bad cultural behaviors due to a lingering gap between the culture as lived and that as communicated. If your instructors use the phrase, "We're supposed to. . . .," you quite likely have a gap.

- **Train all teammates at least annually.** Sustaining your culture requires an ongoing commitment. Sound too expensive? It's not. Culture is everything.

- **Culture should be taught face-to-face in small group settings.** The best way to do this is for the trainers to travel to the work sites. This helps ensure that the training will be completely relevant to the day-to-day work.

- **No PowerPoint.** I'm going to say that again: **No PowerPoint.** If you use visual aids, make them physical and leave them with the people you've trained. This reinforces the concrete nature of the culture. PowerPoint is absolutely useless for this purpose.

- **Train the team to employ peer pressure for the general good.** I've worked in a number of places where safety was considered to be a primary cultural value, yet every time someone had an accident, we found that one of their teammates knew they were engaging in unsafe practices. Use roleplaying to get the team comfortable with calling each other out on cultural violations and correcting them.

- **Listen as well as talk.** Teammates care deeply about their work environment. Give them room to vent, complain, and openly discuss any disconnects between the culture as communicated and as lived. Expect there will be some concern that some people in the company aren't walking the talk. Do *not* attempt to defend anything except the culture itself.

- **Demonstrate personal commitment.** Let the teammates you train know how important the company's culture is to you and why you care about it. I'll never forget the safety director at my company who explained to us why she was so adamant about safety by relating the personal story of a family member who'd wound up with permanent disabilities from driving a forklift off the back of a loading dock late one night.

- **Wherever possible, have your longest-serving employees conduct the training.** Aside from the tremendous credibility they possess and the profound respect other employees have for them, their long-standing commitment sets an example for all to follow. Plus no one will tell better stories about the culture over time than they will.

Recognition

This is a simple but often-overlooked area. What we reward, we will get more of. If we want desirable behaviors to thrive in our workplaces, then we need to reward those behaviors, not once in a blue moon, but every day. A simple "thank you" does wonders when sincerely offered by managers doing their walkarounds. Pick someone every month who has best exemplified the company's cultural values the prior month. Every quarter or year, depending on the size of the organization, give out awards for those teammates who have best lived a cultural value or behavior. Raffle off an attractive prize at the company picnic for those folks who've won a culture award during the year. Create a "Culture Hero" parking space (the plant manager's old spot will do nicely) and let them park there for a month or a quarter. Allow teammates getting top cultural performance marks to choose their shifts, overtime opportunities, vehicles, routes, and/or vacation days first. Keep $100 in the kitty and hand it out each month to the employee you catch in the act of doing something in complete alignment with the culture. For the introverts among us who might be embarrassed by public displays of gratitude, pull them aside in a quiet moment and buy their lunch or present them with a gift card to one of their favorite restaurants or stores. Where you have discretion, reward those consistently living the culture with an extra paid day off, often the most coveted prize of all.

The options are endless, but the effect is the same: demonstrate gratitude toward those employees who have chosen to live the company culture every day they come to work. When such recognition becomes a steady drumbeat, good habits will be forming throughout your organization.

It will also be important to ensure that the company's various recognition programs fully align with the culture. If quality is a key value, we must ensure that performance metrics apply only to quality output and not defects; otherwise, employees will quickly figure out that the company is giving out bonuses to employees who produce big piles of junk. If customer service is a value, you cannot be rewarding call center associates based on how quickly they can dump customers off the phone. In many ways, recognizing people for doing the wrong thing is one of the hardest habits for companies to break, thanks to the long-standing belief that any recognition is good in and of itself.

Time is precious, and one of the most underutilized but powerful forms of recognition comes about simply by making time for someone. At one company for which I worked, as we went through a cultural transformation, the CEO was looking for ways to better support the effort. The Chief Transformation Officer suggested that he make time to personally call and thank teammates who'd epitomized the new culture particularly well. I submitted a colleague based on the West Coast for this honor, provided a short write-up of what he had done, and the CEO used that as talking points when he and the CFO called this young supervisor to praise his conduct. The teammate told me afterward that that was the first time he'd ever talked to a CEO one-on-one and that it was one of the proudest moments of his life. Do you think that particular person continued to excel at demonstrating the new culture's values? You bet he did! Moreover, he told a lot of people about that phone call, which can only have helped sustain the culture. A five-minute phone call from the right person on the right topic can change lives.

Company Functions

If you want to know how well the culture at your company is being lived, keep a close eye on how people behave during company functions. The Christmas Party or Sales Meeting is a place where employees tend to let their hair down toward the end of the event. If your culture is being lived properly, you'll see the same behaviors at 2 a.m. near the swimming pool that you would at 9 a.m. in the conference room. Well, not quite the same, but similar enough.

If your company prides itself on servant leadership, for example, you shouldn't see executives sending interns to the cash bar so they don't have to wait in line. One company I worked for decided to save a bit of money by having junior execs double up on rooms while at the annual company retreat at a resort, while senior execs were allowed to come out a day earlier and with their spouses and families being put up by the company. No doubling up with a stranger for them! That didn't send the message of selfless leadership that was intended.

At another company, the Operations team was driving around downtown Dallas looking for the restaurant where we were all meeting after the first day of the conference. We passed a beautiful, Greek-columned restaurant that looked like the sort of place Gordon Ramsay would own. "Is that it?" I asked. My colleagues laughed. "No, that's where the Sales team is eating. We're eating here," one said, pointing at a rundown taqueria. So much for our teams being on equal terms.

I bring these examples up not to resurrect old gripes but to demonstrate how common and easy it is for companies to undermine their stated cultural values and drive wedges between the culture as communicated and as lived with unforced errors at the worst possible time: when we're all gathering together and reflecting on our culture. A little planning and care could turn these events into showcases for how wonderful our culture is.

One good example of this occurred at the very same company that previously had the Operations folks dine at the Mexican taco shack. We wanted to demonstrate how important the plant managers were to our company, so we created an Old Hollywood theme for the banquet night and literally rolled out the red carpet for the plant managers, complete with some "paparazzi" we'd engaged to ensure they had some headshots commemorating the occasion. This was very well received, as you may imagine, and strengthened the message of the meeting and our culture regarding our field employees. Before we ask others to live our culture, we should live it ourselves first—in everything we do.

The armed forces make great use of tradition to underscore this point. Every year, the Air Force holds a ball in honor of the founding of the service. Toward the end of the evening, cake is served. By tradition, the longest-serving veteran and the youngest airmen come forward to cut the cake together with a saber, symbolizing the unbroken line of service represented by the gap in service time between them. There is always an empty place setting reserved for prisoners of war and those missing in action; this is a constant reminder of the loss felt that they are not attending that night and that any one of their fellow airmen could share their fate tomorrow. It is impossible to leave such an event without the appreciation that you are one of a select few, part of a unique culture outsiders will never fully understand.

We can do the same with our company functions. Take along a memento of the company's founder, or some treasure from the early days. If you don't have time-honored traditions, start some. Offer a toast to a legendary company figure, now passed on. Make up a silly song and teach it to people. Imbue some article of clothing with significance and have everyone wear it. Build a bond between your employees that they won't find anywhere else. Make them feel like they're part of something truly special.

Sustaining your culture requires vigilance, discipline, and constant refinement of processes and organizational structures. Done right, you will plant your culture's roots so deeply within the soil of the company that it will soon be impossible to separate the two. Moreover, you will find that the amount of friction in even large, complex organizations eases considerably as more and more of the work flows naturally with the cultural current.

TWELVE

Who Will Carry the Torch?

"Without memory, there is no culture. Without memory, there would
be no civilization, no society, no future."

—ELIE WEISEL[56]

With the battles of the past behind us, with the proper structural supports put into place throughout the company to nurture and sustain our culture, the work of the first generation of cultural revolutionaries and change agents comes to a close.

Yet much work remains to be done.

The company is constantly changing, buffeted by the howling winds of the marketplace and the capriciousness of governments, challenged by new innovations, pushed and pulled by the turnover of the personnel who comprise the organization. A management fad or three will come along to cause fundamental rethinking of the culture and its values.

If we have built well, the culture will prove remarkably robust down through the years and will require only some fine-tuning in order to stay relevant. If we have built poorly, it will be washed away like so much flotsam and jetsam at the first high tide.

As the men and women who designed the culture move on to other endeavors, it is therefore very important that we pass the cultural torch along to those who will carefully tend its flame. But to whom?

There is great risk in selecting any one person, for none know when fate will intervene and take the ability to perform their duties as keeper of the culture from them before they themselves could select the most suitable successor. Historically, this resulted in the Wars of the Diadochi ("Successors") and the collapse of the vast Greco-Persian empire Alexander the Great had created. Julius Caesar was likewise struck down before he could cement his vision of the

Roman state; a new spate of civil wars broke out which ended the Roman Republic and ushered in the reign of the Roman emperors.

Likewise, entrusting the culture to the entire company, while it has a certain egalitarian virtue, is not going to have any practical benefit in preserving what we have passed down. Ten short years from now the company will look quite different, as the people in it will have substantially changed over time. Having not been through the conformation/reformation/transformation crucible, we can hardly expect them to be as tightly bonded to the principles of the culture formed from the flames as we are.

Therefore, I am going to make one last radical proposal.

But first, a question: In any institution, any organization, any team, who is the most invested in ensuring that values are transmitted and standards maintained? To whom does culture matter most?

Think of your local homeowner's association or town council. Who tends to take part in such activities, willing to sacrifice time and energy to ensure that everyone cuts their lawn or that no one has a serif font on their mailbox?

Once we've gone through all the pitched battles and all the change that was required to give birth to this wonderful culture we've built, who can be counted upon to defend it and resist changes which would erode it? Who will man the battlements and guard the culture, rain or shine, dawn to dusk to dawn?

Is the answer not, "Those who have been here the longest?"

Indeed, aren't those who choose to spend their whole careers with the company not likely to be the ones most deeply committed to its culture?

My radical proposal is this: Form an Old Guard. Create a committee or team that is specifically chartered with maintaining your company's culture. Establish a set number of positions and fill the ranks by tenure with your longest-serving employees. It doesn't matter what roles they have or how degreed they are—all that matters is that they've been around a long time and are committed to the company and its culture. If you've followed previous advice, there will be no danger that someone gets on this council who does not fully believe in the culture we've so carefully erected. Take advantage of this and fill it by age. When someone retires, select the next longest-serving employee.

These should be positions of great honor, and the group should advise senior leadership on cultural matters. The chairperson should get a seat at the senior leadership table; after all, Protector of the Culture is a role essential for the success of the company because culture is everything.

Creating such a team will have the salutary impact of recognizing your most devoted employees, of giving more junior personnel a goal to aspire to in the future, of ensuring that there is constant vigilance in maintaining your culture, and in demonstrating ongoing commitment from the organization to that culture. You may find that in bringing together people from different areas of the company to focus on cultural issues you will also get better ongoing intelligence as to how teammates truly feel about how the company is living out its values.

I've mentioned Napoleon Bonaparte several times in this book, but here again is an area in which he was well ahead of his time. He brought together France's elite troops in his Imperial Guard, culling every formation of its best and brightest in order to form the unit. The most veteran soldiers of the Imperial Guard, those who had seen at least 10 years of Army service, faced enemy fire at the front, and been decorated, were selected for the Old Guard, which was the most prestigious unit in the French Army. These were Napoleon's "grognards," his old soldiers, the men who marched all over Europe in search of glory. They served to inspire the ordinary rank-and-file with their imposing stature (minimum 5'10" at a time when average height was around 5'6") and elaborate uniforms. They were given the exclusive privilege of complaining to the emperor and thereby served the important function of communicating the discontent of the soldiers. They were not thrown into the fray like the line infantry, but rather were held in reserve and used to steady other units on the battlefield, rather like a large rock jutting out of a storm-tossed sea which anchors the fragile vessels in its orbit. When they did fight, it was when the stakes were highest and where the battle would be most decisive; it must have been quite the spectacle to see them march steadily forward toward the enemy, completely unperturbed amid the din and chaos of the battlefield. The other soldiers called them "The Immortals," both in honor of the elite Persian unit from ancient history and in cynical recognition of the fact that their life expectancy was likely much higher due to their fighting so rarely. The Old Guard protected the person of the emperor on the battlefield, a job surely only fit for the most loyal and competent soldiers. They were the mortar that held together the mighty fortress that was Napoleonic France, which is no doubt why their legend lives on after more than two hundred years.[57]

Doesn't your company culture deserve an Old Guard?

Of course it does.

Culture is everything.

APPENDICES

How Culture Relates to Process

We have defined company culture as "the manner by which an organization's values are communicated, understood, and lived by its members," and further described it as the way the company does what it needs to do. Process improvement practitioners may have a question in mind, "How does the company's culture impact its business processes?" It is this question that the author will endeavor to address in this section of the appendix.

Let's establish the critical relationships first and then describe how they interrelate. **Leadership** defines what the company's **strategy** is and further defines the **vision, missions, goals, objectives,** and **organizational structure** necessary in order to get there. Further, leadership defines the **values, norms,** and **behaviors** desired in order to efficiently and effectively execute the strategy. The former is the What, Where, When, and the Why; the latter is the How.

Strategy and culture then should equally inform the design of our business processes. We must establish processes which are capable when properly executed of delivering the results the business expects, both in terms of bringing the company closer to realizing its strategic vision and doing so in a way that is consistent with the company's values. If we wind up further away from accomplishing our goals or if we hit the number but compromise our shared values or engage in undesirable behaviors to do so, we will have failed.

As process improvement professionals, we live in the center of this model, constantly battling to figure out how the company can improve execution and deliver ever-greater business results. We tend to treat the top half of the model as mere prerequisites for success, which in practical terms means it is a useful scapegoat for when projects fail. As experts in root cause analysis, of course, we really ought to dig a little deeper and understand the strategic and cultural reasons why our efforts to improve processes in a given area didn't reach their full potential. Here are some common causes from the Strategy and Culture buckets:

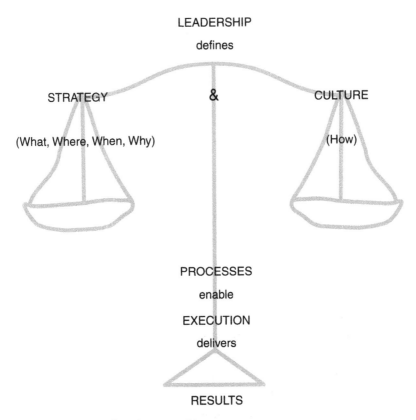

LEADERSHIP

defines

STRATEGY   &   CULTURE

(What, Where, When, Why)   (How)

PROCESSES

enable

EXECUTION

delivers

RESULTS

FIGURE 36. How culture interacts with process

- Strategy
  - The company's vision wasn't bold enough relative to its mission.
  - The company's mission was unclearly defined.
  - The company's mission does not reflect operational reality.
  - When taken as a whole, the company's goals did not close enough of the gap to the vision for significant business results to be achieved.
  - When taken as a whole, the company's objectives did not close enough of the gap to fulfill the goal.
  - The company's metrics were poorly defined, thereby making the barometer of business results unreliable.
  - The company's strategy was not effectively time-bound, lacking urgency.

- Culture
  - The company's values did not sufficiently enable its strategy (e.g., "customer comes first" and "people are our most important asset" conflict at face value; which has the priority?).
  - The company's values are lacking something essential to achieving its strategy.
  - The company's values are slogans without sufficient definition.
  - The company's desired behaviors do not align with its values (e.g., "collaboration" and "teamwork" as values, while desired behavior is "stay in your lane."
  - The company's desired behaviors make it much more difficult to achieve objectives and goals.
  - The company's culture is not clearly communicated.
  - The company's culture is not clearly understood.
  - The company's culture is clearly communicated and understood but not being lived.

Diagnosing these causes in project postmortems/lessons learned/mission debriefing sessions can be very helpful in understanding the constraints involved in process design or reengineering. Processes need to run with the grain of the company culture and toward achievement of the company's strategic vision, maintaining the precarious balance shown in the model above.

An example may drive this concept home.

Apple is the most admired company in the world for 2019 according to *Fortune* magazine.[58] Apple's mission statement is as follows:

"Apple designs Macs, the best personal computers in the world, along with OS X, iLife, iWork and professional software. Apple leads the digital music revolution with its iPods and iTunes online store. Apple has reinvented the mobile phone with its revolutionary iPhone and App store, and is defining the future of mobile media and computing devices with iPad."[59]

Its vision as articulated by CEO Tim Cook is:

"We believe that we are on the face of the earth to make great products and that's not changing. We are constantly focusing on innovating. We believe in the simple not the complex. We believe that we need to own and control the primary technologies behind the products that we make, and participate only in markets where we can make a significant contribution. We believe in saying no to thousands of projects, so that we can really focus on the few that are truly important and meaningful to us. We believe in deep collaboration and cross-pollination of our groups, which allow us to innovate in a way that others cannot. And frankly, we don't settle for anything less than excellence in every group in the company, and we have the self-honesty to admit when we're wrong and the courage to change. And I think regardless of who is in what job those values are so embedded in this company that Apple will do extremely well."[60]

Apple's cultural values (inferred) include:

- Excellence
- Creativity
- Innovation
- Secrecy
- Combativeness[61]

Apple's publicly stated cultural values include:

- Environment
- Supplier Responsibility
- Accessibility
- Privacy
- Inclusion and Diversity[62]

Given this, we can see that Apple is in transition from a computer manufacturer to a device manufacturer and is deeply committed to cutting-edge innovation. Apple will succeed so long as the company maintains its position on the bleeding edge of sophisticated devices which are easy to use.

Some of the company's values directly enable the drive toward its vision. Hiring the very best people in the technology sector (excellence), creating a world-class working environment for creatives (creativity), constantly developing new products (innovation), preserving their proprietary technology (secrecy), and being willing to engage in project Darwinism to ensure that resources flow to the best ideas (combativeness) all comport well with what the company is trying to do. The public values tend to work as constraints with regard to achieving the stated goals: concern for the environment, limiting supply-chain options based on how well they treat their employees, preserving accessibility for disabled users, protecting the privacy of users' information, and hiring practices based on factors other than pure competence in one's field tend to slow or limit progress toward the company's objectives.[63]

In designing business processes at Apple, therefore, we need to first bear in mind what it is the company is trying to do, then incorporate how it would like to do it through the company's values.

You've just been hired by Apple with the express mandate to completely over-haul Apple Stores. These are the retail spaces where Apple sells its products while customers wait for their devices to be repaired or ask personnel questions about them. In preparing to take on this task, you pull together the following scorecard:

Category	Grade
Innovation	B
Simplicity	D
Significant market contribution	C
Excellence	B
Creativity	D
Secrecy	C
Combativeness	F
Environment	D
Supplier Responsibility	C
Accessibility	F
Privacy	F
Inclusion and Diversity	B

FIGURE 37. Apple Store scorecard example

These are pretty dismal results, all things concerned. While the architecture of the Apple Stores and the commitment to essentially hide product inventory in stockrooms were once innovative, the Apple Store experience has devolved into the equivalent of browsing Best Buy shelves while waiting for the Geek Squad technical support team to fix your device. Long lines are the norm, and appointments are necessary to avoid excessive wait times. The stores tend to be present in major urban areas and cater to this clientele, preventing the opportunity to make a more significant contribution by reaching those outside of the young, hip, dual-income, no-children demographic. Moreover, the sheer number of people packed into an Apple Store makes it a nightmare from a privacy perspective. The overall experience is anything but simple; you essentially have to take a number and wait until a harried representative can spare a few precious minutes to understand your problem and route you to the next person. A process resembling the typical government bureau's queue or a waiting room at the doctor's office isn't going to earn high marks given Apple's high standards.

A process redesign for the Apple Store, therefore, should feature a customer experience that is simple, accessible, and personal. In America, Starbucks is the ubiquitous coffee shop and Walmart the most expansive retail chain. Why not partner with them to place small Apple Store footprints within their facilities? Where customer volume is still high and driving wait times, why not loan waiting customers the next generation of devices they have or new devices they might want to try? That way they could play with it while waiting or browsing other stores. Let them sign up for an initial 10-minute diagnostic session at a kiosk or online, turn over their device as necessary, then notify them on the loaner device that their device is ready. Partner with local online retailers to hold most of the inventory, allowing footprints to be very small. Perhaps courier delivery could be utilized to drop off repaired and new purchases at the customer's home, preventing the need for them to wait around. Perhaps Apple could schedule focus groups during waits, increasing engagement and allowing customers to play a greater role in innovation by soliciting their feedback on the loaner devices.

The combativeness value is an interesting one to accommodate. It is an essentially Darwinian approach to innovation in which the best ideas win. Perhaps this could be applied in the Apple Store context by requiring solutions to be collaborative, although this may water down innovation and stretch resources needed to deliver excellence even thinner.

The solution above may not make us millions of dollars in stock options bestowed upon us by a grateful board at Apple, but it's illustrative of the way in which strategy and culture should inform process design. We want business processes that are going to help the company get where we need to go in the manner we desire to get there. This means we cannot simply develop or reengineer these processes looking only at the immediate impact upon customers and teammates within the process; we must keep our eyes on bigger prizes yet.

Once business processes have been properly aligned with what the company is trying to accomplish and with the company culture, we have set these processes up for success. They will run with the strategic and cultural grain, encounter much less cultural impedance, and facilitate execution. This in turn will magnify the positive business results these processes were designed to deliver.

Grading Scales for Cultural Dimensions

Within the body of this book we introduce six dimensions of culture that are most useful to diagnosing and defining desired cultural behaviors in the process improvement/Lean context. Of course, there are many more contexts that are applicable to this approach, which in turn leads to the definition of additional cultural dimensions. I have included some additional objective scales below that may prove useful.

Customer Focus (CF) Dimension Objective Scale

Rating	Criteria
5	Customer experience is the primary focus of all employees at all levels of the company.
4	Customer experience is the primary focus of top-level management.
3	Customer experience is the primary focus of sales management.
2	Customer experience is the primary focus of customer-facing employees.
1	There is no evidence of company focus on the customer's experience.

Decision Authority (DA) Dimension Objective Scale

Rating	Criteria
5	Where decisions are in contradiction between two decision-makers, the more credible decision-maker always wins.
4	Where decisions are in contradiction between two decision-makers, the more credible decision-maker usually wins.
3	Decisions are made by balancing organizational rank and credibility.
2	Where decisions are in contradiction between two decision-makers, the higher-ranking decision-maker usually wins.
1	Where decisions are in contradiction between two decision-makers, the higher-ranking decision-maker always wins.

Decision-Makers (DM) Dimension Objective Scale

Rating	Criteria
5	Employees at the lowest level of organizational hierarchy are fully empowered to stop production, satisfy customers, employ company resources, and manage risk at their discretion.
4	Supervisors and above are fully empowered to stop production, satisfy customers, employ company resources, and manage risk at their discretion.
3	Managers and above are fully empowered to stop production, satisfy customers, employ company resources, and manage risk at their discretion.
2	Junior executives are fully empowered to stop production, satisfy customers, employ company resources, and manage risk at their discretion.
1	Senior executives are fully empowered to stop production, satisfy customers, employ company resources, and manage risk at their discretion.

Decisive Information (DI) Dimension Objective Scale

Rating	Criteria
5	Where data contradicts experience, data always wins.
4	Where data contradicts experience, data usually wins.
3	Decisions are made by balancing data and experience.
2	Where experience contradicts data, experience usually wins.
1	Where experience contradicts data, experience always wins.

Driver of Change (CD) Dimension Objective Scale

Rating	Criteria
5	Change originates with the employees performing the work.
4	Change originates with middle management.
3	Change originates with the company's top leadership.
2	Change originates with external consultants.
1	Change originates with market, regulatory, supply chain, or customer pressures.

Innovation Accountability (IA) Dimension Objective Scale

Rating	Criteria
5	Employees at all levels of the organization have specific performance objectives involving innovation.
4	Mid-level managers have specific performance objectives involving innovation.
3	Top-level managers have specific performance objectives involving innovation.
2	Top-level managers have performance objectives involving innovation.
1	There is no evidence of accountability to innovate.

Innovation Collaboration (IC) Dimension Objective Scale

Rating	Criteria
5	All innovation teams are self-generated, and participation is determined by employees self-nominating.
4	Most innovation teams (50%+) are self-generated, and employees are selected to participate by their supervisors.
3	Some innovation teams are self-generated, and employees are selected to participate by their supervisors.
2	Innovation teams are formed by mid-level management.
1	Innovation teams are formed by top-level management or do not exist.

Innovation Scope (IS) Dimension Objective Scale

Rating	Criteria
5	Innovation occurs throughout all areas of the company and its supply chain.
4	Innovation occurs throughout the company.
3	Innovation occurs in parts of the company directly related to products and services the company offers as well as in enabling business processes.
2	Innovation occurs in parts of the company directly related to products and services the company offers.
1	Innovation occurs only at the highest levels of the company and with regard to the company's business model and strategy.

Lean Focus (LF) Dimension Objective Scale

Rating	Criteria
5	Reducing waste is the primary focus of all employees at all levels of the company.
4	Reducing waste is the primary focus of top-level management.
3	Reducing waste is the primary focus of operations management.
2	Reducing waste is the primary focus of customer-facing employees.
1	There is no evidence of company focus on reducing waste.

Magnitude of Change (CM) Dimension Objective Scale

Rating	Criteria
5	The majority of employees embrace major changes in the company's products, services, policies, processes, and strategies.
4	The majority of employees embrace minor changes in the company's products, services, policies, processes, and strategies.
3	The majority of employees neither resist nor embrace major changes in the company's products, services, policies, processes, and strategies.
2	The majority of employees resist major changes in the company's products, services, policies, processes, and strategies.
1	The majority of employees resist minor changes in the company's products, services, policies, processes, and strategies.

Pace of Change (CP) Dimension Objective Scale

Rating	Criteria
5	Employees expect core job functions to change more frequently than once per month.
4	Employees expect core job functions to change approximately once per month.
3	Employees expect core job functions to change approximately once per quarter.
2	Employees expect core job functions to change approximately once per year.
1	Employees expect core job functions to change less frequently than once per year.

Process Management (PM) Dimension Objective Scale

Rating	Criteria
5	Standards prominently displayed for all significant tasks and compliance is 80%+ OR process mistake-proofed so that deviation from standard is not possible.
4	Documented standards prominently displayed for all significant tasks, but compliance is 80% or less with these standards.
3	Documented standards prominently displayed for all significant tasks, but compliance is 50% or less with these standards.
2	Documented standards exist but are neither displayed nor deliberately followed.
1	No evidence of documented standards in workplace.

Quality Focus (QF) Dimension Objective Scale

Rating	Criteria
5	Quality is the primary focus of all employees at all levels of the company.
4	Quality is the primary focus of top-level management.
3	Quality is the primary focus of operations management.
2	Quality is the primary focus of customer-facing employees.
1	There is no evidence of company focus on quality.

Cultural Archetypes Associated with Process Improvement

Much of this book has been concerned with the application of six defined cultural dimensions related to process improvement to characterize different cultural archetypes that the reader may find useful. I've previously focused on the ten most relevant of these archetypes. The full list is provided below.

Dimension	Definition
Decision-Makers (DM)	How dispersed decision-making authority regarding process is across the company. Where teammates are very empowered, there will be many decision-makers; where process control is highly centralized, there will be few decision-makers.
Decisive Information (DI)	What type of information is prized and determinative in making decisions within the organization. Numbers-driven cultures will score high for quantitative information; gut-driven cultures will score high for qualitative information. Where both are present, select the type which in the end the decision-maker(s) will use to come to a final conclusion.
Decision Authority (DA)	How decision-making authority is defined. In hierarchical organizations like the military, rank or positional authority determines who decides; in startup companies or virtual organizations, credibility and knowledge will be determinative.
Pace of Change (CP)	How often process change is desired within a company. This will range from static environments where the status quo is to be protected to dynamic workplaces where the status quo is to be disrupted.
Magnitude of Change (CM)	How large a desired change may be and still be supported by most within an organization. This may run from tiny, incremental improvements to fundamental redesigns of how we work. This represents the appetite for change.

Dimension	Definition
Driver of Change (CD)	Where the impetus for change comes from. In externally focused cultures, it comes from outside (usually customer, sometimes market or regulatory). In internally focused cultures, it comes from within the four walls of the company.

NOTE: If you take exception to the labels the author has placed upon these archetypes, feel free to replace with ones more agreeable to you. These are intended to be descriptive, not dogmatic.

Name	DM	DI	DA	CP	CM	CD	Description
Aristocratic	1	1	1	1	1	1	A culture at the opposite end of Anarchic in each dimension; distinguished by a strong hierarchy with strong traditional bent and highly resistant to change.
Founding	1	1	1	1	1	5	A culture that has a strong tradition and resists change, but where employees are greatly empowered, similar to a mature startup/very small firm.
Corrective	1	1	1	1	5	1	A culture that is largely stagnant, but the employees yearn for change.
Compliant	1	1	1	1	5	5	A culture where change happens slowly, but in an orderly fashion when it does, and tends toward sweeping change on these occasions.
Farming	1	1	1	5	1	1	A culture in which small changes happen very often but otherwise is very traditional.
Conforming	1	1	1	5	1	5	A culture in which individuals constantly make small changes in order to conform with the strategic direction of the company.
Torch-Passing	1	1	1	5	5	1	A culture undergoing large shifts quickly, such as when the torch is passed from a founder to a successor.
Revolutionary	1	1	1	5	5	5	A culture undergoing large amounts of change driven by an elite.

(continued)

Name	DM	DI	DA	CP	CM	CD	Description
Expert-Driven	1	1	5	1	1	1	A culture where change is driven by a small elite of subject matter experts. This is typical of Silicon Valley companies.
Operations	1	1	5	1	1	5	A culture that is a meritocracy resistant to change, but very focused on customer (and sometimes regulatory) requirements.
Opportunistic	1	1	5	1	5	1	A culture in which large changes are made by a small elite as they spot opportunities for positive change.
Venture Capitalist	1	1	5	1	5	5	A culture featuring large changes made by expert employees as they see opportunities.
Scientific	1	1	5	5	1	1	A culture wherein highly skilled employees initiate small changes frequently.
Architecting	1	1	5	5	1	5	A culture featuring frequent small changes from a wide variety of employees.
Turnaround	1	1	5	5	5	1	A culture that is internally focused, undergoing frequent, substantial change, guided by a few insiders.
Entrepreneurial	1	1	5	5	5	5	A culture wherein a small elite make many large changes based on their gut feel for the business.
Guarding	1	5	1	1	1	1	A data-driven culture which is highly change resistant.
Tactical	1	5	1	1	1	5	A culture that changes slowly based on data and the initiative of employees on the front line.
Ponderous	1	5	1	1	5	1	A culture featuring large changes made sporadically based on compelling data.
Big Game Hunting	1	5	1	1	5	5	A data-driven culture wherein frontline employees can trigger large changes.
Perfecting	1	5	1	5	1	1	A data-driven culture in which small changes are frequent.
Tailoring	1	5	1	5	1	5	A data-driven culture featuring lots of small changes made by experts.

(continued)

Name	DM	DI	DA	CP	CM	CD	Description
Strategic	1	5	1	5	5	1	A data-driven culture wherein employees welcome large, frequent changes made by leadership.
Visionary	1	5	1	5	5	5	A data-driven culture in which large changes are frequently initiated by all levels of the company.
Six Sigma	1	5	5	1	1	1	A culture featuring strong leadership control combined with continuous incremental improvement driven by data.
Engineering	1	5	5	1	1	5	A culture that is designed and redesigned based on the expertise of an elite few.
Innovating	1	5	5	1	5	1	A data-driven culture wherein large changes can be initiated by credible employees within the organization.
Marketing	1	5	5	1	5	5	A data-driven culture allowing large changes to infrequently be initiated by employees at all levels within the organization.
Inventing	1	5	5	5	1	1	A data-driven culture in which processes are constantly being tinkered with.
Regulating	1	5	5	5	1	5	A data-driven culture featuring small, frequent changes made by top leaders driven by employees at all levels.
Designing	1	5	5	5	5	1	A data-driven culture featuring small, frequent changes made by top leaders driven by external factors.
Consulting	1	5	5	5	5	5	A data-driven culture featuring large, frequent changes made by top leaders.
Feudalistic	5	1	1	1	1	1	A culture featuring strong employee empowerment, but otherwise highly resistant to change.
Managerial	5	1	1	1	1	5	A culture featuring strong employee empowerment combined with a voice in making floor-level changes, but is also change averse in general.
Guiding	5	1	1	1	5	1	A culture featuring strong employee empowerment and infrequent, large, externally driven change.

(continued)

Name	DM	DI	DA	CP	CM	CD	Description
Building	5	1	1	1	5	5	A culture featuring strong employee empowerment and infrequent, large, employee-initiated change.
Ownership	5	1	1	5	1	1	A culture featuring strong employee empowerment and frequent, small, externally driven changes; typical of single-owner privately held companies.
Stewardship	5	1	1	5	1	5	A culture featuring strong employee empowerment and frequent, small, employee-initiated changes; typical of single-owner privately held companies.
Prophetic	5	1	1	5	5	1	A culture featuring strong employee empowerment and frequent large, externally driven changes with decision-making based on gut feel and experience rather than data.
Patriarchal	5	1	1	5	5	5	A culture featuring strong employee empowerment and frequent large changes based on the credibility of the individual making the decision; based on gut feel rather than data.
Accounting	5	1	5	1	1	1	A culture featuring strong employee empowerment and few small, externally driven changes based on credibility.
Lawgiving	5	1	5	1	1	5	A culture featuring strong employee empowerment, credibility-based, internally initiated, infrequent small changes.
Culture-Building	5	1	5	1	5	1	A culture featuring strong employee empowerment, large, infrequent, externally driven change driven by credible leaders.
Empire-Building	5	1	5	1	5	5	A culture featuring strong employee empowerment, decision-making based on experience, and infrequent, large, internally driven changes.
Customer Service-Oriented	5	1	5	5	1	1	A culture featuring strong employee empowerment, gut-level decision-making based on credibility, and frequent small changes driven by external events.

(continued)

Name	DM	DI	DA	CP	CM	CD	Description
Sales-Oriented	5	1	5	5	1	5	A culture featuring strong employee empowerment, decision-making by gut feel and based on credibility, with frequent, small, internally driven change.
Creative	5	1	5	5	5	1	A culture featuring strong employee empowerment, decisions made by gut feel and based on external input, with frequent, large changes.
Dreaming	5	1	5	5	5	5	A culture featuring strong employee empowerment, decisions made by gut feel and internally driven, with frequent, large changes.
Caretaking	5	5	1	1	1	1	A culture featuring strong employee empowerment, data-driven, hierarchical decision-making, and infrequent small, externally driven changes.
Governing	5	5	1	1	1	5	A culture featuring strong employee empowerment, data-driven, hierarchical decision-making, and infrequent small, internally driven change.
Statesmanlike	5	5	1	1	5	1	A culture featuring strong employee empowerment, data-driven, hierarchical decision-making, and infrequent, large, externally driven change.
Chairman	5	5	1	1	5	5	A culture featuring strong employee empowerment, data-driven, hierarchical decision-making, and infrequent, large, internally driven change.
Legislative	5	5	1	5	1	1	A culture featuring strong employee empowerment, data-driven, hierarchical decision-making, and frequent small, externally driven change.
Lobbyist	5	5	1	5	1	5	A culture featuring strong employee empowerment, data-driven, hierarchical decision-making, and frequent, small, internally driven change.
Activist	5	5	1	5	5	1	A culture featuring strong employee empowerment, data-driven, hierarchical decision-making, and frequent, large, internally driven change.

(continued)

Name	DM	DI	DA	CP	CM	CD	Description
Change Agent-Driven	5	5	1	5	5	5	A culture featuring strong employee empowerment, data-driven and hierarchical decision-making, where large, frequent, internally driven change happens.
Tribalist	5	5	5	1	1	1	A culture that is both loosely controlled (lots of tribes and chiefs) and highly resistant to change, only engaging in such when external events so dictate. Decision-making authority is credibility based.
Technocratic	5	5	5	1	1	5	A culture featuring strong employee empowerment, data-driven decision-making, where small, internally initiated changes happen infrequently. Typical of environments with tightly integrated systems.
Planning	5	5	5	1	5	1	A culture featuring strong employee empowerment, data-driven decision-making, where big, externally driven change happens periodically. Typical of many banks today.
Coaching	5	5	5	1	5	5	A culture featuring strong employee empowerment, data-driven, credibility based, but conservative when it comes to the pace of change.
Lean	5	5	5	5	1	1	A culture in which everyone plays a part in incremental improvement of the company through the reduction of waste.
Service	5	5	5	5	1	5	A culture featuring strong employee empowerment, data-driven decision-making with credibility prized, and frequent small changes.
Libertarian	5	5	5	5	5	1	A culture featuring strong employee empowerment where change is driven by external factors.
Anarchic	5	5	5	5	5	5	A culture with extremely decentralized decision-making and constant, significant change; akin to a brand-new startup.

FIGURE 38. Cultural dimension definitions and cultural archetypes associated with process improvement

Culture Change and Company Size

How does the approach to culture change differ depending on the size of the company? Would a startup be handled differently than a globe-spanning conglomerate that has been in business for over a century?

Startups and small companies have the advantage of greater flexibility in establishing or reforming a culture. By necessity, employees in these types of enterprises must generally cover more ground and interact with wider swaths of the organization than do their more compartmentalized compadres in big companies. If just a few of these employees start behaving differently, a large portion of the culture changes for good or ill. Moreover, small-firm employees tend to have access to more information about the company, rather like neighbors in small towns do. This means that they are likelier sooner to comprehend changes in market winds necessitating cultural change than their large-firm counterparts.

The process outlined in the preceding chapters could be tweaked in light of the smaller scope of the startup and small company:

- Greater emphasis should be placed on designing the proper culture rather than letting it grow without tending.
- The first employees are the germ of the much larger company's leadership; do not let anyone fill the ranks who is not an ideal fit for the desired culture, or you could buy yourself decades of problems.
- Factions grow as the company grows; keep employees connected through the culture to limit potential dysfunction later.
- Smaller, fast-paced operations resist bureaucracy and standardization; emphasize attitude and cultural alignment to ensure that as processes get put in place, they will be reasonably aligned with culture.

- A smaller cast of characters combined with a fast-paced environment makes for terrific founding myths—be sure to capture these "war stories" from the early days to inspire people later on.
- Smaller organizations tend to be more cohesive and tolerate candid feedback better; use this to your advantage when including cultural feedback and accountability in operating routines.
- Do not overemphasize formality and documentation in these environments; it is counterproductive, as there is more natural resistance to both.
- Qualitative methods of assessment work very well in smaller operations, where it is easy to observe the behaviors of all.
- If someone is not adding positively to the culture, take action swiftly before large portions of the company are negatively affected.
- Burning platforms for change are generally much easier to build in these types of companies due to less security and more of a tendency to rally together in tough times; this makes it a lot easier to begin the necessary changes.
- Personal relationships being stronger in smaller companies, heightened empathy in providing critical feedback or in terminating employees is wise, so as to avoid the rest of the employees having a negative view of leadership and the culture.
- Hypocrisy is absolutely devastating in such small organizations. If anyone fails to follow through and live the values of the culture, they must be dealt with severely or employees will quickly lose confidence in the culture.

Large companies, by contrast, by their very size, geographic scope, and complexity, can hardly be said to have any one homogenous culture at all. Cultural assessments performed in large companies should therefore stratify results by geographic region and country; chances are this data will show that the results for culture as communicated, understood, and lived will be significantly different across this dimension. Likewise, operations that were recently acquired ought to be evaluated separately as the legacy company culture may hold out for quite some time.

In addition, the following tweaks to the general approach in this book ought to be considered when dealing with large companies:

- More effort will need to be expended on standardization with commensurately less tolerance for deviation from cultural norms.

- Senior leadership needs to be especially cohesive. It may be better for this reason to replace leadership at the edges of the company with leaders absolutely loyal to the culture from within the core of it.
- Take advantage of training, conferences, and other meetings where employees are brought to a central location for a common purpose. A culture discussion line item on the agenda can pay big dividends in increasing cultural cohesion.
- Large companies often have the resources to build and maintain centralized training for all employees. Push for an equivalent-sized culture center and have it handle training programs related to culture. If that isn't possible, cultural training ought to comprise a significant part of the training center's agenda.
- More employees means more cultural heroes—providing effort is made to identify them and share their stories across the company.
- In larger organizations, politics and the general disconnectedness of employees erode trust and may make candid cultural feedback hard to come by. Create safe spaces where functional and dysfunctional aspects of the culture may be discussed freely, preferably without identifying who raised concerns.
- To ensure standardization in messaging around culture, write it down.
- In evaluating the culture in larger companies, the emphasis should be on quantifiable results so as to make valid comparisons between sites and regions.
- The sheer size of the operation often means more flexibility in dealing with recalcitrant culture holdouts; it takes longer for them to convert sufficient quantities of other employees to jeopardize the culture. This provides an opportunity to coach them or remove them quietly.
- In big companies, burning platforms for change must be huge. With a big enough challenge, though, great gains in cohesion can be made as employees rally to fight a common foe.
- The widespread use of written policies in larger firms can be a wonderful help in ensuring that personnel are in alignment with the company's culture; simply ensure that the desired behaviors are defined within the policy, and then strictly enforce it.
- Senior leaders in particular must live the values of the culture. Nothing so cements the credibility of the culture than when a senior leader known to have broken faith with it is swiftly shown the door. The reason, barring some tremendously embarrassing incident, ought to be made public to reinforce the message.

- Due to the heightened visibility of large-company leaders in the media, it is very important that they make a habit of talking about the company's culture in interviews. This will not only demonstrate true commitment to the company's employees, but will also make it easier to recruit talent to the company that is already sympathetic to the prevailing culture.
- Wherever possible, align cultures up the supply chain. After all, should your vendor cut any ethical corners, the news sites will run headlines saying "Company X's Vendor . . ." Work with suppliers you can trust because they share your values. Perform your cultural assessment at their facilities.

While company size is certainly a consideration, it chiefly impacts how we operate only on the margins. Whether your company is tiny or enormous, with some very minor alterations you can successfully apply the approaches described in this book and achieve much stronger alignment with your desired culture as a result. As with all we do with regard to company culture, it requires some planning, analysis, innovation, communication—and quite a bit of good, hard work in the execution of it.

Generational Implications of Culture Change

With the advent of the millennials, much cultural navel-gazing has ensued in conference rooms regarding the need to find ways to accommodate this strange new group of people in the workforce. I sat in on one of these myself during talent planning at a large, well-established Fortune 500 company. We had a lengthy discussion regarding how to attract and retain this particular demographic, including changes required of managers in order to prevent millennials from fleeing the company. It was an odd discussion, to say the least, for this Gen Xer; at one point I had to ask, "Do you think management had this discussion when we were coming up?" Everyone laughed; of course not, we were expected to conform to the company culture, not the other way around.

This is not to knock millennials. It is not their fault that the "snowflake" narrative has stuck to their generation any more than it is mine that the "slacker" narrative stuck to mine. In many ways, and certainly for many individuals, these generational narratives are unjust. How is a coward who dodged the WWII draft covered in the same "Greatest Generation" glory as one of the Rangers who scaled La Pointe du Hoc on D-Day? The very notion is ridiculous.

That said, we simply cannot ignore the fact that our workforce is comprised of people at very different stages of life, with different life experiences and often conflicting values, even when these people come from the same geographic areas. In crafting company cultures, we are essentially asking these very different people to embrace and live the same set of values, even where they may conflict with deeply held personal beliefs. For these efforts to be successful, the desired culture must be one which employees of all generations can rally around.

A few years ago (okay, it was 17; it seems like yesterday to me), I worked for another Fortune 500 company. Our Vice President of Manufacturing refused to communicate via e-mail. Instead, he would have his administrative assistant print out all of his e-mails. He would write handwritten replies which she would then type up and send. This laborious process went on day after day. He was a smart man and not ignorant of emerging technologies, particularly as related to the manufacturing of consumer products; he just didn't want to take the precious time to learn something that new and of dubious value to him at that point in his career.

That calculation impacts many of our older workers. Technologies come and go. Making an investment in mastering WordStar early in your career may have made a lot more sense than doing the same with Microsoft Word 2013 much later in it, if only because you won't be using the latter for as long before retirement. There is also the natural aversion to revisiting old problems to consider. We've often experienced considerable success using certain tools to solve problems earlier in our careers. It feels like going back to square one to revisit them using new methods which may have not yet proven to work from our point of view. Why waste time when we already have a proven solution? I live this each day now as a Six Sigma Master Black Belt, Six Sigma having gone into eclipse with the collapse of GE.

I've noted elsewhere in this book how longer-tenured employees become the natural guardians of company cultures and are absolutely vital to the success of any culture change effort. It is because we tend to be the most resistant to cultural change that we in effect become the company's immune system, hunting down and destroying infectious agents.

Of course, change agents could elect to simply wait us out. We won't be here forever, after all, and there will be fewer of the Old Guard to contend with each and every year. This is precisely how some companies deal with labor unions. They save their ammunition at contract time for ensuring that no new, young union members are brought in while largely ameliorating the concerns of the aging union workforce. It has been a very successful strategy for companies with the wherewithal to be patient and wait decades. That is probably not an option for companies in crisis.

A better approach would be to identify those areas that are most essential to culture change and sweeten the pot for tenured employees who embrace them. This is the situation that proponents of 401(k) retirement savings matching in the United States faced some years ago. The previous regime of generous pensions paid out after 20–30 years of continuous service was unsustainable at many companies, and the Social Security government program would be unlikely to preserve retirees in anything resembling their old lifestyles as life expectancy improved and retirements became longer. How do you get employees with a short time until retirement to put away additional funds for retirement? You play on their fears that Social Security will not be there or that the company will be compelled to cut pensions at some point and sweeten the pot with "free money" through the company match, typically a capped percentage of salary dependent upon how much employees choose to put into the 401(k) account. You also make 401(k)s portable, reducing the risk of the employee losing retirement benefits should they be laid off by the company.

That same approach can help get tenured employees on board with the new culture. Address the fear and positively reward those who embrace the new way of doing things.

The most junior employees represent different challenges, in no small part because they want different things than more senior employees do. Flexibility, mobility, work-life balance, exciting work, time off, and personal growth opportunities tend to resonate with this demographic more than it does with their predecessors, who tend to be more focused on pay, benefits, and opportunities to take on more responsibility.

I ran into this stark difference in values myself when working with a process engineer I'd recruited to my team. He was briliant, creative, and sociable; and I thought I had hit a home run professionally when he came aboard. I gave him a challenging assignment and supported him as I would have liked to be supported, with no micromanagement and plenty of room to learn on the job. He left to take a job in the software world that allowed him to spend about half his time in Florida (we were based in Virginia). He told me I reminded him of his father and that he found the environment too constraining, something I'd failed to pick up on during our many conversations. It was nothing personal and we stayed in contact for some years afterward; he simply sought a culture which was more conducive to the life he wanted to live, a decision for which I can do nothing but applaud him. As you can see from this book, I came to agree with his approach, and fear I learned more from him than he ever did from me.

A similar phenomenon is at work in the current battle over the workplace. Younger workers have grown up with social media and information technology and find the notion of the company town completely alien. They are more sensitive to the various indignities involved in daily commutes and generally do not wish to have to compromise living where they want to live for a job in an era where telecommuting is so easy. Some companies have addressed this by making workplaces hipper and more pleasant than the cube farms I spent most of my career laboring within. Even those senior managers who successfully transitioned to e-mail, instant messaging, and teleconferences have struggled with managing teams where individuals only come into physical contact a few times a year. The old model of "out of sight, out of mind," though completely discredited, has proven attractive to many of us seeking to preserve the illusion of control. The tighter we cling to it, the more we will alienate younger workers, especially those talented individuals who mislike signs of distrust from their managers.

I worked from home for about five years while a banker, despite living in the same city as our headquarters. I'd long considered the move but feared taking it due to backlash from senior leadership. I finally took the plunge when my manager shocked us by revealing to us he had spent the last six months working from his home two hours away from the office and no one on the team had even noticed. I had a very young and growing family at the time, and working from home dramatically increased the amount of time I could spend helping my wife out at home and interacting with my young children. I found it very difficult to unplug from work, however, and over time wound up working far more hours at home than I had when I went into the office, which led to my eventually taking a job with a commute and my presence strictly required in the office. Having the flexibility to select an arrangement that worked best for the company, my family, and myself was an absolute blessing. I relay this personal anecdote because I think I can better appreciate the perspective of my younger colleagues, having had this experience myself.

This also points the way to ensuring that our new culture meets the needs of employees. In addition to being able to attract and retain younger teammates through flexible work arrangements, these also tend to save money, boost company loyalty, and significantly increase productivity. Since experiencing work-from-home and hoteling approaches to work, I regularly tell my folks, "I don't care where you do your work. I care about the value you produce and the way in which you produce it." I am willing to concede a 9-to-5 workday (well, more like 6-to-6 for me most days) and the satisfaction of seeing my team slugging away at the problems of the day for the boost to morale and productivity we get from this. I believe that many senior leaders would do the same merely by appealing to business results and the welfare of our people. A nice side benefit has been that

I no longer desire a big corner office, the classic corporate status symbol. It is so much better to be able to be productive anywhere.

Another cultural difference between workplace generations involves recognition. In my career, I have typically been motivated by promotion, raises, and increased responsibility along with the occasional award. These typically involve annual performance reviews. The business world has shifted more toward the desires of the younger generation for more frequent and informal feedback, mentoring, and the award of time off and simple "thank you's." As organizations have become flatter and more collaborative, this evolution will no doubt continue. When I have discussions with my manager, I now tend to ask for permission to tackle the biggest, ugliest problems the business has, chiefly because solving these gives me the greatest professional satisfaction. This is generally a much easier discussion to have than to ask for a loftier title (titles are increasingly meaningless) or more money, which tends to take care of itself once you solve a couple of these big, ugly problems most sane people prefer to avoid. I tend to be embarrassed by praise, and I'm sure I'm not alone. One terrific direct report I had was a strong introvert and very strongly preferred additional time off (she suffered from migraine headaches which were very debilitating and very unpredictable; my way of saying "Great job!" soon became "Take the day and recover," which she appreciated. If we can provide the flexibility within our culture to reward people in the way that they—not we in management—value most, it should be a lot easier to attract and retain top talent.

In sum, if we want a company culture that is actually lived by employees at all levels of the organization, we should endeavor to craft and communicate that culture in a fashion which enhances its appeal to all employees. Much as we did earlier in soliciting particular individuals and groups for support for the new culture, we should target our efforts appropriately to maximize this appeal by offering enough of interest to these demographic segments as to make their adoption of the new culture easier. We must show flexibility, particularly in areas that may improve the company's ability to achieve its strategic vision, trading off a little bit of additional change against much higher levels of buy-in. Seek out opportunities that benefit all (even if in different ways), as these are the most impactful.

Efforts made to make the new culture more livable by teammates at all levels can only help to improve the prospects of the company in embracing the desired culture and therefore aid in the realization of the company's vision.

International Implications

I am an American, born and raised. My writing therefore stems from my experiences as an American businessman of the late twentieth/early twenty-first centuries; it could not be otherwise. As such, it is certainly a valid criticism of this work to this point that it may not have full relevance and application in cultures other than my own.

Fortunately, I've had occasion to travel internationally throughout my military and business careers and have seen firsthand some of the differences between cultures in several countries on several continents and that of the U.S. I am by no means an expert on international cultures, surely, but hope that my experience plus some old-fashioned research will make this particular appendix useful to those engaged in international business.

We'll take each of the largest and most influential cultural groupings in turn and provide insights in order to tailor portions of the processes which are desirable for American companies but less so for companies operating under different flags.

Asia

Business is personal in Asia. Before there can be a business relationship, there must be a personal relationship, one built on mutual respect and honor. Business leaders tend to be lower-profile and less boisterous than their American counterparts, evoking a quiet dignity. The pace of change is generally slow, and great deference is shown to hierarchy. In making changes, particularly personnel changes, great care must be taken to allow for impacted personnel to save face. Employees generally feel more communal responsibility to the company than in America, a difference clearly seen in the apology rituals in some Asian countries, where public apologies are made following big business mistakes. Turnover is typically much lower than in America, and loyalty to the company is very much expected. Recognition tends to be less individualized and far less showy in Asia.

Here are some implications for cultural change in Asia:

- Any criticism of the current culture must be made very subtly and obliquely.
- Politeness is extremely important in Asia; it is essential to closely watch what people do rather than what they say during assessments.
- Change must begin from the top of the organization.
- It is best whenever possible to allow leadership within Asian organizations to drive change there, rather than have outsiders attempt to drive it.
- It will take longer to implement change.
- Always allow for your Asian business partners to save face.[64]
- Big changes require deep trust—build that trust first.
- Conform will be a successful strategy far more often than Reform and Transform will.
- Emphasize the benefits to society of changes.

Europe

Despite the relative similarities between American and European cultures, there are still some minefields to be navigated in driving culture change with our Old World colleagues. Labor unions are a much stronger presence in Europe than in America, which can make culture change slower and more difficult to achieve. Bureaucracies are larger and the regulatory environment much more demanding than in the U.S. Terminating employees is far more difficult and disruptive. Europeans tend to identify less with their employers than Asians or Americans do. Business ownership structure is typically more complex. Ostentatious displays of wealth are generally frowned upon. Political and historical stories, jokes, and discussion is generally fraught and should be avoided. Manners are typically more formal.

What does this imply for our approach to cultural change?

- Change will typically take longer and take a more circuitous route than in America.
- Changes will generally require a higher level of documentation due to the labor and regulatory environments.

- Changes should be discussed in the context of impact on the company and society as a whole; "WIIFM" gets far less traction in Europe than in America.
- Communications should be precise, detailed, and multilingual (English, French, Spanish, German, and Italian, at least).
- Dress down as a general rule for European audiences; no power suits and Rolexes.
- Avoid uses of historical or political analogies when explaining culture change to Europeans, so as to limit controversies.[65]
- Always start from a position of mutual respect when dealing with European colleagues.
- Body language and behaviors vary widely across Europe; rely on local experts to help inform your cultural assessments.

Africa

Africans on the whole are more formal and respectful of hierarchy than their American counterparts. It is important to show proper respect to superiors, those with titles, and the elderly in particular. Decision-making is more consensus based and can be relied upon to take longer than in the U.S. Like Asia, relationships are important, and one should expect to build up personal relationships before transforming them into business relationships. Interactions tend toward formality.

When pursuing culture change in Africa, it would be wise to:

- Be cognizant of the hierarchies involved and endeavor to respect them.
- Introduce changes at the top of hierarchies and leave time for them to discuss with their teams.
- Leave plenty of time for follow-ups, as decisions can take awhile.
- Do not expect that lower-level employees will be candid with you, especially about problems; instead, strive to develop a relationship with the top person in the hierarchy.
- As Africans tend to strongly favor the communal over the individual, be sure to couch benefits of the new culture and detriments of the current culture in terms applicable to the whole organization or community.
- Condescension is particularly frowned upon, so be sure that communications are open, transparent, and do not come off as arrogant.

- Avoid sharply criticizing the current culture, and instead focus on the wonderful things the new culture will bring to all.

Latin America

Latin American culture has similarities to European culture (so much of the influence upon it having come from the Iberian Peninsula historically), but there are some important differences as well. Latin Americans tend to be less formal with regard to punctuality and meeting agendas but more formal in attire, largely because status is important. Like other regions, in Latin America personal relationships precede business relationships; deals may not happen if the parties do not have a good personal relationship. Latin Americans typically favor strong family bonds and identify secondarily with their companies. In similar fashion to Asian cultures, it is typically wise to allow Latin Americans to save face in less pleasant situations.

- Respect hierarchies when communicating change; it is generally resented to communicate to subordinates before their leaders.
- Be sure to know which employees have familial ties, as this may complicate efforts to change the culture.
- Break out those power suits and Rolexes—status symbols matter, particularly for outsiders.
- When discussing culture change, keep the emphasis on how we will build the wonderful new culture together, and avoid discussing the past culture to avoid offending employees.
- Your authority may be tested during the process—do not hesitate to assert it, firmly but politely.
- Privilege the personal over the professional by engaging in criticism privately and diplomatically.
- Always afford the higher person in the hierarchy the opportunity and time to learn new behaviors and skills first, privately whenever possible.

Middle East

Honor and respect are enormously important to most Middle Easterners. Negotiations and decision-making are much slower than in America. The personal and professional worlds of Middle Easterners overlap nearly completely, each person in effect acting as a web of networked contacts with cultures that operate on lines more akin to "who you know" than "what you know." Favors are exchanged as a matter of course, and one gives to get. The strong family bonds typical of the region mean that even if the person assents in the meeting to your request, they may need to demur to clear it with higher-ranking family members, or to seek their consensus. These are face-saving cultures; it is vital to avoid direct criticism. Written correspondence may be more candid. As with Latin America, status symbols such as clothing or jewelry may be helpful.

Given these considerations, the following suggestions are offered:

- Cultural transformations are highly unlikely to succeed; try whenever possible to adopt a Conform strategy given the likelihood of extreme resistance.
- Be very aware of hierarchy and carefully defer to it.
- Enlist a reliable guide to the web of relationships you will need to navigate.
- Avoid criticism and negative language ("opportunities" rather than "defects" or "problems," etc.).
- When criticism is unavoidable, do so obliquely and in private and allow your interlocutor to save face.
- Emphasize observable behavior strongly in assessments; employees are highly unlikely to be candid.
- Leverage animosities when you can—there is often a history between key players and sometimes a bad one. This can be turned to your advantage.
- Change management will be a give-and-take; expect to compromise during implementation.
- Allow plenty of time for changes to be adopted; the pace is generally far slower in the region than Americans are accustomed to.
- Collaboration will be undertaken along the strict lines of hierarchy; do not expect to see self-forming teams and the like.
- Include give-and-take in your stakeholder analyses; identify what each stakeholder really desires in return for supporting the effort, and do your best to provide it.
- Bureaucracy is powerful within this part of the world and often a key to getting and maintaining status. Follow its requirements meticulously until one of your contacts is able to bring about a shortcut based on their relationships.

For our purposes, Australia, New Zealand, and Canada may be addressed in similar fashion to Europe. Other nations may best be addressed as a combination of two or more regional cultures, as might be the case with Indonesia and Malaysia (Asian + Middle Eastern, due to the Muslim influence).

With a bit of savvy tailoring, the general approach outlined in this book should prove fruitful for most engagements across the world. Think of the regional culture as a superset of the company culture to which a Conform strategy is always required. Flexibility and innovation will help practitioners move closer to desired cultures so long as we do not run too strongly against the grain of the national culture.

Culture and Job Searches

How does the principle "Culture Is Everything" apply to those seeking jobs, rather than companies seeking workers?

Just as we advise recruiters and hiring managers to prize cultural fit above everything else, so too do we recommend that job-seekers look first and foremost for the cultures they best fit and most desire to be part of, before role, title, salary, benefits, industry, and location. Culture is the primary concern because it will determine how likely you are to love your job—and whether or not your job will love you back. Find the right culture and work becomes virtually effortless and fun; find the wrong one and no matter how good a fit you are for the role, you will struggle mightily just to remain marginally acceptable to your new employer.

How do we find the right company culture for us?

1. **Know yourself.** You need to perform a self-assessment in order to uncover your strengths and desires. Two tools which I have found exceptionally useful (well worth a Duck Duck Go search) are Strengths Finder 2.0 and the Keirsey Temperament Sorter. The former will provide insight into the work behaviors which come most naturally to you, and the latter will provide insight into your personality and how it meshes with others. Stop trying to cover your weaknesses; embrace your strengths instead.

2. **Know which culture you thrive in.** This book provides you with the framework of cultural dimensions defined by a quantified behavioral spectrum. You can apply this framework to define your desired culture. Take your Top 5 strengths from the StrengthsFinder assessment and combine with the key preferences from your Keirsey results to create a 5-category spectrum for each top strength. For example, if you are strong in Command with an ENTJ (Field Marshal) personality type, build a dimension called Span of Control and a 5-point scale from

Individual Contributor to Senior Executive, which will help you assess whether your positional authority is sufficient to leverage your Command strength and your need to be in charge.

3. **Know the company.** Once you have your dimensional spectra defined, add a column for each target company on your wish list and turn it into a scorecard. Then do your homework. Many companies maintain online presences which speak to their culture (culture as communicated). Mine this first to provide scores in the dimensions of interest to you. Next, leverage your network via LinkedIn and other social media to identify anyone you know (or who knows somebody you know) who can answer some specific questions as to how the company lives out these dimensions, updating your scorecard accordingly. Use these initial scores to whittle your target company list down to those likely to have acceptable cultures; then apply for roles available there. Once you get into your interviews, probe for how the culture is actually lived by asking questions of your interviewers and observing your surroundings. If you're a deliberative ISTJ, you will want to feel like everything is well organized, orderly, and calm.

4. **Know the role.** Once you're comfortable that you've locked onto the right company culture for you, then—and only then—should you scrutinize the role. You're seeking at this point to maximize the culture score. Say, for example, that you're a learner INFJ, but the role as currently constructed doesn't allow you enough access to different types of people to help. Can the role be expanded to allow for this? Can responsibilities be shifted from other roles? Can you periodically augment another area where such contact is the norm? If so, this may greatly increase your satisfaction with and prospects for success in the role.

This simple process can greatly improve the odds that you land in the company with the most fertile soil for your professional growth.

Hang on to the scorecards you've developed, though. If at some point you find yourself swimming against the current in your new company, use these scorecards to reassess how the culture is being lived. If it has drifted away from you, and if there are no plans to reform or transform it, you will want to begin your job search again.

In this way, the cultural barometer we have built will help you stay ahead of events, furthering your career and potentially saving you stress, worry, and negative financial consequences. Use your scorecards as a sort of early-warning radar to help you manage your career and maximize your happiness.

At different stages in your career, your strengths and personality may shift slightly, particularly in those categories which were on the edge of two buckets quantitatively, so be sure to take the assessments again every couple of decades and reassess what you need from a company in order to fully thrive. This is also a good exercise to undertake, because as we get older and amass a wealth of experience, we tend to do so at the expense of our early flexibility—at some point the concrete of our personality and preferences does set. If we find the perfect work environment by the time this hardening occurs, we will have been very fortunate indeed.

The "Culture Is Everything" Approach to Cultural Change

The practical application of the principles outlined in this book are important. Although cultural change is by its nature strategic work, the work breakdown structure below may prove useful to anyone seeking to close the gap between theory and reality.

	Step
1.	Clarify what your company must do.
1.1.	Define your vision.
1.2.	Define your mission.
1.3.	Define your values.
1.4.	Define your goals.
2.	Define the dimensions of the company culture that will best enable your company to achieve its goals while honoring its values, fulfilling its mission, and attaining its vision.
2.1.	If improving quality is one of your primary objectives, you can use the six cultural dimensions defined in Chapter 5 in lieu of defining your own.
2.2.	For other cultural dimensions, seek to expand upon your values by identifying desirable and undesirable behaviors to fill in the 5-point objective scale.
2.3.	Cross-check dimensions to ensure they do not overlap one another. Behaviors should be unique to one dimension.
2.4.	Establish a desired score on the objective scale for each dimension.
3.	Assess your current culture against the desired culture.
3.1.	Develop a survey instrument.
3.1.1.	Include similar questions for each major area—Communicated, Understood, Lived.

(continued)

	Step
3.1.2.	Word questions neutrally and use a Likert scale to quantify a response based upon strength of agreement/disagreement. Include a "neither agree nor disagree" bucket—apathy means something!
3.1.3.	Analyze the results, looking not just at the mean responses but the outliers. Were any parts of your organization significantly better or worse than others? Since you have defined the most desirable results, you can compare how different each response is from that result, much as you would do during a Bias Study when applying Gauge R&R or Measurement System Analysis.
3.2.	Conduct a focus group.
3.2.1.	Gather a representative, random sample of employees.
3.2.2.	Prepare a questionnaire similar to the survey instrument described in 3.1.
3.2.3.	Ask focus group each question, seeking a consensus rating. Discuss any outliers.
3.2.4.	Analyze the results in similar fashion to 3.13 above. Include any observations from the facilitator which sheds light on the discussion.
3.3.	Conduct a culture audit.
3.3.1.	Establish two-person audit teams.
3.3.2.	Develop the audit instrument, which should consist of the objective scales for all relevant dimensions with some commentary around grading them.
3.3.3.	Have each audit team observe the activities of an area of interest (a team, site, or division) for 1–2 days, independently assessing behaviors witnessed for alignment to desired cultural behaviors.
3.3.4.	Have each team review results together to arrive at a consensus rating for that area.
3.4.	Conduct interviews.
3.4.1.	Develop an interview questionnaire similar to that described in 3.1.
3.4.2.	Interview senior leaders for how they would grade the company in each dimensional area.
3.4.3.	Interview key customers (largest, longest-lasting, most important) as to how they would grade the company in each area.
3.4.4.	Interview key suppliers (largest, longest-lasting, most important) as to how they would grade the company in each area.
3.5.	Aggregate and report results to senior leadership.
3.5.1.	Explain the scoring system and instruments.

(continued)

	Step
3.5.2.	Provide overall results, bucketed by As Desired, As Communicated, As Understood, and As Lived.
3.5.3.	Discuss biggest gaps between each bucket first.
3.5.4.	Discuss results by demographic slices.
3.5.5.	Describe the best of the best and worst of the worst in concrete terms to ensure buy-in to the results.
4.	Develop a cultural change strategy.
4.1.	Complete a Risk vs. Effort Matrix to understand which strategy is best suited for your company's situation.
4.2.	For each cultural change strategy, review the pros and cons associated with it.
4.3.	Solicit the support of the top person in the company for the favored strategy.
5.	Implement strategy to Conform (if favored).
5.1.	Conduct a deep dive on the cultural assessment results to identify the largest differences between current and desired culture.
5.2.	Identify the biggest levers to pull associated with bridging the gap between current and desired culture. This may be a person, a policy, a process, a team, a function, or a site. Develop and implement a strategy to move this lever the right way.
5.3.	Broadcast the results from this gap-closing effort in a way which positively reflects the current culture.
5.4.	Reward the new behavior(s) and punish the old.
6.	Implement strategy to Reform (if favored).
6.1.	Complete the Readiness for Cultural Reform Questionnaire. If not ready, adopt a Conform strategy instead.
6.2.	Assemble the true believers.
6.2.1.	Complete a stakeholder analysis to identify those most and least likely to support the cultural change.
6.2.2.	Develop and implement a strategy to influence key personnel.
6.2.3.	Recruit those with most enthusiastic support for the effort to the team.
6.2.4.	Bond the team together in opposition to the current culture.
6.3.	Build the movement.
6.3.1.	Develop a recruitment strategy.
6.3.2.	Engage recruitment targets one-on-one.

(continued)

	Step
6.3.3.	Motivate new recruits to help change the current culture.
6.4.	Undermine the status quo.
6.4.1.	Conduct a SWOT analysis to exploit the current culture's weaknesses and magnify threats to it.
6.4.2.	Choose best targets to undermine.
6.4.3.	Develop and implement strategy for sustained attack on the current culture.
6.5.	Win and keep winning.
6.5.1.	Absorb new recruits to effort.
6.5.2.	Sustain pressure on the current culture.
6.5.3.	When tipping point is reached, formally implement desired culture.
7.	Implement strategy to Transform (if favored).
7.1.	Complete the Readiness for Cultural Transformation questionnaire. If not ready, adopt Reform strategy instead.
7.2.	Assemble list of requirements for top leader in company. If not adopted, adopt Reform strategy instead.
7.3.	Assemble the transformation team.
7.4.	Conduct a deep-dive review of the current company situation using the Company Current State Questionnaire.
7.5.	Publicly defy the old culture.
7.5.1.	Identify a key opportunity to condemn the current behaviors.
7.5.2.	Forcefully oppose the current culture and carefully observe the reaction.
7.6.	Develop prioritized list of additional cultural improvement opportunities by populating the Cultural Opportunity Assessment Matrix.
7.7.	Assimilate the organization into the desired culture, leveraging the Cultural Opportunity Assessment Matrix list.
7.7.1.	Train teammates on desired cultural norms and behaviors.
7.7.2.	Provide opportunities for teammates to apply these norms and behaviors.
7.7.3.	Reinforce positive behaviors and criticize negative ones.
7.8.	Grow the desired culture.
7.8.1.	Identify potential guardians of the desired culture.

(continued)

	Step
7.8.2.	Neutralize remaining opponents of the desired culture.
7.8.3.	Purge the old culture from business processes.
7.8.4.	Fully incorporate the desired culture into people-related policies and procedures.
8.	Sustain the desired culture.
8.1.	Craft a founding myth.
8.2.	Implement metrics to track how well the desired culture has been communicated and understood and how well it is being lived.
8.3.	Incorporate cultural health into operating routines.
8.4.	Incorporate support for the culture into performance management.
8.5.	Incorporate cultural fit into hiring and firing decisions.
8.6.	Incorporate cultural values and sustainability into business process design.
8.7.	Align project management routines with cultural sustainability.
8.8.	Train new hires and all employees on culture periodically.
8.9.	Recognize cultural heroes.
8.10.	Align company functions with culture.
9.	Pass the torch to the next generation of culture warriors.

FIGURE 39. The "Culture Is Everything" approach to cultural change

Following this process and using the tools provided should greatly improve the odds of success for a change in culture and thereby improve the chances for process improvements to succeed. The process is neither quick nor easy, but following it will make the Herculean task of changing the direction of a company's culture a bit easier to pull off.

AFTERWORD

Culture is everything.

Culture is the manner by which an organization's values are communicated, understood, and lived by its members. Culture is the set of values and behavioral norms which allow the company to fully accomplish its mission and realize its vision. Cultural information is transmitted via memes.

Some cultures are more suitable than others for companies to achieve their objectives. Company performance can be approved by selecting the most appropriate culture, then adopting a deliberate strategy to conform to, reform, or transform the current culture, and/or reduce any extant gaps between the desired culture and how it is lived day by day.

Once culture is fully aligned with organizational purpose, constant vigilance and nurturing institutions are required to sustain the culture and allow it to remain in lockstep with the company's strategy.

That, Dear Reader, is the simple and clear argument of this book, all half-a-page of it. The remaining hundreds of pages exist to convince you of the truth of this argument and to provide you with detailed guidance as to how to use this information to unleash your company's full potential. The constant resort to personal experiences, historical anecdotes, analogies, metaphors, and bad jokes served to mask the fact that so much of the discussion involves repeating the same principles over and over again in different ways, building up a coherent view of the entire argument in much the same way a 3D printer builds a toy up. It was not simply a case of the author's long-windedness.

I have been a quality and operations professional for over 25 years at the time of this writing. I've worked for seven companies ranging from a couple dozen up to tens of thousands of employees across diverse industries. I've coached and executed hundreds of projects. I've labored in companies with great cultures for process improvement and companies with awful cultures for process improvement and have had success in both.

The sum total of the knowledge acquired in my lifetime in the quality trenches is this: If you want to achieve all that you can achieve, if you want to do truly great things, you must go where the culture is conducive to it. Culture is everything.

That's the business secret I've learned at great cost. It is the professional truth which has set me free.

And now, I have shared it with you.

I have thus discharged my duty to you, my colleague, my reader, my friend, but in doing so I have charged you with a great burden: you must do something with this insight. You and I are going to change business culture one company at a time, transforming barren rock into lush gardens wherein the seeds of quality can be planted and flourish. All it takes is the courage to try.

Will you do it?

Will you take the wisdom contained within the covers of this very reasonably priced and elegantly designed book and apply it at your company, or with your clients, or even to your job search? Will you share your secret knowledge with others who can be trusted to do the same?

The limitations of this medium prevent me from hearing your reply, but my hope is that you will. If you do, you'll have done your part to change the world for the better.

Thank you for your patient indulgence and perseverance unto

THE END

ENDNOTES

1. Jim Collins, *Good to Great* (New York: HarperCollins, Inc., 2001).

2. Nassim Nicholas, Taleb, *The Black Swan: The Impact of the Highly Improbable* (New York: Random House, 2007).

3. Retrieved from https://www.brainyquote.com/quotes/leah_busque_727240 on 8/2/18

4. The question as to how far one may stretch the notion of an organization's members from a cultural point of view is a good one. Companies like Toyota and Apple have very strong cultures, and the penumbra extends through contractors and even into the supply chain. I generally view culture as being first and foremost a product of how employees do their jobs under the influence of their leadership. The sourcing and supply-chain implications of culture are addressed in Appendix D.

5. A note of caution to the reader: There will be *many* anecdotes in this book, historical, professional, and personal. The author has developed the bothersome habit of explaining concepts by recourse to analogy, a practice which some will no doubt find tiresome, particularly if the subject of the analogy is of little interest to them. There was a character on the NBC sitcom *Cheers* some years ago who was famously annoying for making asides which demonstrated his knowledge of trivia. That is not my intention, but I can't resist working in some military history here and there.

6. This has never actually happened to the author, but man, does he wish it had.

7. Taylor Swift is not, in fact, a great quality philosopher.

8. This has happened quite often to the author. Fate is a cruel mistress.

9. This is a reference to the wonderful film *The Sound of Music*.

10. Retrieved from https://www.brainyquote.com/quotes/jeff_bezos_449991 on 8/2/18

11. Not that we don't try to automate bad processes from time to time. There's a reason that old saw exists: "When we automate a bad process, we just get more defects faster."

12. There is a fourth—culture as leadership defines it, and even a fifth—culture as customers experience it; these may be relevant at times and are worth noting.

13. I've chosen these labels from political history in an effort to keep them as value-neutral as possible; while some may be preferable from the standpoint of a Lean or quality culture, all are valid and have their strengths in certain industries and at certain stages of company development. These labels are therefore descriptive but not judgmental.

14. Retrieved from https://blog.enplug.com/37-company-culture-quotes on 8/10/18

15. Retrieved from https://blog.enplug.com/37-company-culture-quotes on 8/15/19

16. If there is one change which would dramatically improve American companies' ability to compete, it would be to do this very thing. Once employees no longer have to fear the layoff ax, they naturally begin seeking ways to make their jobs easier.

17. Retrieved from https://www.linkedin.com/pulse/leading-change-why-70-transformation-programs-fail-d-suryawanshi/ on 9/4/19

18. Joseph M. Duran and Joseph A. DeFeo, editors, *Juran's Quality Handbook,* 6th Edition (New York: McGraw-Hill Education, 2010), 301–302.

19. Michael L. George, *Lean Six Sigma: Combining Six Sigma Quality with Lean Speed* (New York: McGraw-Hill Education, 2002), 17.

20. Anthony Manos and Chad Vincent, editors, *The Lean Handbook: A Guide to the Bronze Certification Body of Knowledge* (Milwaukee, WI: Quality Press), 3, 278–289.

21. This strategic focus necessitates giving up on other opportunities, which no doubt will lead to champions of those initiatives to leave the company. This is addition by subtraction and should not be feared.

22. Retrieved from https://www.brainyquote.com/quotes/steve_blank_800234 on 8/2/18

23. Retrieved from https://www.zappos.com/about/what-we-live-by on 7/21/19

24. Who should ask such questions? Anyone interested in the answers.

25. Note that while there is a quantitative element to such assessments, we are more interested in the movement over time in the ratings (either toward or away from desired behavior) than carrying a result to the fifth decimal place. Indeed, if a number is heading the right way but concerned parties don't feel that improvement in their bones, feel free to take action anyway. This will be more productive than a Gauge R&R on the survey instrument is likely to be.

26. Retrieved from https://www.azquotes.com/quote/1380473?ref=culture-change on 7/21/19

27. If you haven't read *Quality Is Free*, you really must. If W. Edwards Deming sometimes comes across as a grumpy uncle giving a lecture, Crosby is like taking a car ride to Disneyland with Zig Ziglar. It is a balm for the quality engineer's soul.

28. Retrieved from https://www.dictionary.com/browse/meme on 7/26/19.

29. Chip and Dan Heath, *Why Some Ideas Survive and Others Die* (New York: Random House, 2007).

30. Retrieved from https://www.history.com/this-day-in-history/washington -puts-an-end-to-the-newburgh-conspiracy on 7/26/19

31. Retrieved from http://transmissionsmedia.com/the-inexplicable-precision -in-the-construction-of-the-great-pyramid-at-giza/ on 7/28/19

32. Malcolm Gladwell, *The Tipping Point: How Little Things Can Make a Big Difference*. (Boston: Little, Brown, and Company, 2000).

33. Retrieved from https://www.azquotes.com/quote/401052?ref=fork-in-the -road on 7/29/19

34. Retrieved from https://www.linkedin.com/pulse/leading-change-why-70 -transformation-programs-fail-d-suryawanshi/ on 8/2/19

35. Retrieved from https://www.brainyquote.com/quotes/peter_drucker_130601 on 8/2/18

36. Retrieved from https://www.goodreads.com/author/quotes/1771.Sun_Tzu on 7/30/19

37. Retrieved from https://www.poetryfoundation.org/poems/56968/speech -friends-romans-countrymen-lend-me-your-ears on 7/30/19

38. Retrieved from https://www.brainyquote.com/quotes/christopher_bond _167898?src=t_reform on 7/30/19

39. I kid.

40. Retrieved from https://www.azquotes.com/quote/182933?ref=culture-change on 8/3/19

41. This term came from the best episode of Patrick McGoohan's peerless TV show, *The Prisoner*, entitled "Once Upon A Time." It is well worth a watch, especially if you want to appreciate how stressful a cultural transformation can be.

42. Retrieved from https://www.thoughtco.com/blood-toil-tears-and-sweat -winston-churchill-1779309 on 8/3/19

43. Retrieved from https://winstonchurchill.org/resources/speeches/1941-1945 -war-leader/give-us-the-tools/ on 9/5/19. The International Churchill Society is a wonderful organization dedicated to keeping alive the memory of the second-greatest person in history, Sir Winston Churchill. The author highly recommends this organization.

44. Louis V. Gerstner, Jr., *Who Says Elephants Can't Dance? Inside IBM's Historic Turnaround* (New York: Harper Business, 2003), 43.

45. Retrieved from https://medium.com/@shahmm/ibms-turnaround-under -lou-gerstner-case-study-business-management-lessons-a0dcce04612d on 8/4/19

46. Retrieved from https://www.ibm.com/developerworks/rational/library /2071-pdf.pdf on 8/4/19. on 8/4/19. The truly delightful thing about this quote is it is taken from a book review under a section the author entitled— wait for it—"Culture Is Everything." A year into writing this book, I find someone has used its title! I therefore present this reference not simply to give credit where credit is due but to advertise.

47. The author finds this an especially painful admission, as an Oakland Raiders fan.

48. This point cannot be overstated: not everyone will make it through the transition to the new culture. That is reality.

49. *MAD* readers will immediately think of the work of Jack Davis. The illustration in question could have been done by him.

50. Retrieved from https://en.wikipedia.org/wiki/John_Paul_Jones on 8/5/19. We can all learn much from Jones's tenacity and courage, even though we're not dodging cannonballs, musket rounds, slashing sabers, and falling timbers the way he was at the time.

51. "Voluntold" is an Air Force term for forcing someone into service after a "request for volunteers" goes unanswered. The Air Force has a saying: "Never volunteer"; this results in the creation of many honored "Voluntold."

52. Some would claim that title belongs to *The Iliad*. These people are known as "Wrong."

53. Retrieved from https://www.storyboardthat.com/articles/e/heroic-journey on 8/6/19

54. Quality "grognards" will recognize what an awful pun this is.

55. Retrieved from https://www.denofgeek.com/us/books-comics/marvel/243710 /how-marvel-went-from-bankruptcy-to-billions on 8/6/19. This article is referenced chiefly for names and dates; the opinions expressed in my analysis remain my own and do not reflect those of the author of the article.

56. Retrieved from https://www.brainyquote.com/quotes/elie_wiesel_451199 on 8/9/19

57. Retrieved from https://militaryhistorynow.com/2018/11/27/napoleons-old -guard-10-amazing-facts-about-the-french-emperors-legendary-soldiers/ on 8/9/19

58. Retrieved from https://www.msn.com/en-ph/travel/news/the-worlds-most -admired-companies-in-2019/ss-BBT4aPS on 8/26/19/

59. Retrieved from http://panmore.com/apple-mission-statement-vision-state ment on 8/26/19

60. Ibid.

61. Retrieved from http://panmore.com/apple-inc-organizational-culture-features -implications on 8/26/19

62. Retrieved from https://www.apple.com/sitemap/ on 8/26/19

63. Some readers may see this as controversial or as a value judgment being made on company values which are more societal than economical. Engineers in the audience will recognize that constraints are not necessarily bad but simply define the design envelope, much as when a car designer has to account for fuel efficiency even in vehicles whose drivers do not make that a top concern. Companies are free to hire diverse job candidates, for example, and in many if not most cases in the technology sector, it is not difficult to find top talent which qualifies as "diverse" from this perspective. It is simply a fact that ANY criterion beyond technical competence—from not hiring

convicted felons to not offering relocation benefits for a given position—will effectively constrain the desire to hire the best possible talent. Ted Kaczynski was by all accounts a brilliant mathematician; his role outside of work as the Unabomber made him unsuitable for employment no matter how gifted he was. Excluding terrorists from employment, while arguably a constraint, is certainly a very good thing.

64. I really stepped in it with a Korean supplier once. As supplier quality manager for my company, I was sharing audit results with the CEO and his staff. I didn't make allowance for the saving of face with some of the findings, and he grew angry enough to slam his fist on the table at one point. From his perspective, I was personally insulting him by bluntly discussing failings of the company in front of the group. I should in retrospect have discussed them more diplomatically with him in a one-on-one.

65. The author fears he has done those readers with a need to address European teams a disservice with all of the historical anecdotes in the book. Wherever you can get away with it, replacing the name of these historical figures with characters from *Eastenders* may prove wise.

ACKNOWLEDGMENTS

Writing is lonely work, but the writer is never truly alone in the endeavor.

I'd like to thank my wife, Anita, for listening to me act out audio excerpts from the manuscript and for her encouragement throughout the year of this book's writing. Thanks also to Winston, Sophia, and Christopher for letting Daddy alone to write; and to Clementine for never leaving Daddy alone, particularly when he needed a hug.

Thanks to Sharon Woodhouse, Quality Press editor extraordinaire, who has been unfailingly professional, helpful, and supportive throughout this process. Thanks as well to Linda Kast, the wonderful editor who informed me that ASQ wished to move forward with this project and who shepherded me through the middle stages of the process, and to Paul O'Mara, the former ASQ editor who inspired me to begin this project through our long association where I reviewed proposals and manuscripts from a technical perspective. Thanks also to fellow ASQ senior member and author James Bossert, whose enthusiasm for Quality Press and willingness to share his own experience encouraged me to proceed at a critical juncture.

There are many, many colleagues who unknowingly contributed to this book, chiefly by providing much of its anecdotal fodder, but also for the many hallway and breakroom conversations down the years as the idea germinated, sprouted, and eventually flourished. I would be remiss not to name them here; any omissions are a reflection of the author's fallible memory and not of their impact on him: Brett Jordan, Mike Sale, Casey Hofmann, Bryan Cooper, Gordon Kurczyk, Adam Charron, Frank Kvietok, Ben Madden, Jonah Levine, John Utter, Eric Laurance, Jerry Natzke, Luann Lafreniere, Mitch Lehn, Bob Giberson, Rick Brown IV, Ken Miranda, Mike Fath, George Koshy, Geoff Marlatt, Josh Pucci, Tony Nicol, Amy Kovas, Mark Fisher, Kerry Fleming, Chris Sheehan, Carl Hayslett, Matt Porter, Jennie Sandy, Ron Smarsh, Larry Dilworth, Jeff Hollywood, Kim Starke, Cody Phipps, Eric Moeller, Ken Novacich, Kyle Schneider, Tom

Reagan, Julia Boyd, Victoria Rickman, Emily Howell, Rachel McCue, Pete Hofmann, Todd Logan, Greg Labas, Raj Saxena, Faheem Zuberi, Ginger Henderson, Dia Browning, Ralph Browning, Chris Fleenor, Sharyn Fleenor, Tracey Wolsko, Beth Sullivan, Jennifer Owens, Katrina Teague, Dave Weaver, Don Carlson, Bill English, Henrik Mortensen, Judi Melton, Brian Walters, Tamar Dorna, Tapan Pandya, Bob Harris, Tony Green, Laura Tran, Emily Meredith Sledge, John Gilbert, Brian Burdette, Andy Abranches, Scott Thompson, Don Wood, Martin Hairston, Ann Thompson, Barb Vetter, Bob Reagle, Martin Ottenbrite, Ray Daines, Steve Graybeal, Masa Okada, Kurt Lesser, Dave Roland, Ken Sandifer, Juan Rocha, Gloria Lewis, Dave Van de Ven, Yashpaul Dogra, Quentin Tse, Wes Heiman, Dick Boettner, Glenn Korhorn, Jack Bain, Gene Degraphenreid, Steve Kaighen, Bart Enos, John Curcio, Harun Yesin, Clarence Hucks, Roger Hudson, Eric Basile, Eden Merrifield, Dawn Zepeda, Mark Nolte, Ray Campbell, Bill Campos, Dean Judge, Rollie Rupp, Kit Sung, Melanie Oberg, Amy Yeckley, Rob Cioppa, Tom Haynes, John Culpepper, Chris Oleksa, Jeanne Hardrath.

There are also family and friends who have been supportive of my writing and must be thanked lest the karmic blowback diminish sales:

George Veyera, Barbara Veyera, Michael Veyera, Bob Veyera, Gary Veyera, Paula Durette, Diane Driscoll, Pat Maloney, David Voigt, Sue Neufeld, Chuck Stevens, Ben Malisow, Jim Fabio, Jim Woodhead, Mike Meyer, Steve Scherzer, Matt Smith, Dave Nicklaus, Scott Koons, Glenn Roettger, Dennis Showalter, Hank Buck. My number one cheerleader has been my lovely bride, Anita, followed closely by my kids: Winston, Sophia Bella, Christopher, and Clementine.

I would also like to express my deep gratitude to the ASQ reviewers who patiently pored over the manuscript and provided invaluable feedback which greatly improved the final product. When it comes to living their culture, ASQ walks the talk.

INDEX

Note: Page numbers followed by *f* refer to figures. Note information is indicated by page numbers followed by n and note number.

A

ABOUT THE AUTHOR

Jeff Veyera's introduction to the quality profession came as a junior second lieutenant in the United States Air Force when he was "voluntold" to take on the task of heading up the 325th Logistics Group's new Quality Support Office. After the requisite reading of the Deming, Crosby, and Juran quality corpus and a pilgrimage to the Quality Air Force epicenter at Maxwell AFB, AL, he began teaching and preaching the principles of process improvement. In his next assignment as a Fuels Management flight commander in Misawa, Japan, Veyera decided to apply strategic planning principles to his new operation, which led directly to the complete turnaround of the flight's culture and it being recognized by The American Petroleum Institute as the Best Fuels Management Flight in the Air Force. This was the moment Veyera became a quality zealot.

In his post-military career, Veyera worked for some of the most prestigious companies in America, displaying a remarkable ability to show up at precisely the moment the company or industry was turned upside down. He joined GE at the outset of the Six Sigma and global sourcing revolutions, leaving just as his division president was elevated to CEO for a telecom startup that was a casualty of the tech sector collapse of 2001. He ran supplier quality at Black & Decker at the moment the company struggled to balance global sourcing opportunities with the new demands of the hassle-free return culture of big box retailers. His tenure at Bank of America, which began applying quality controls to the data warehouse environment, was bisected almost perfectly by the financial crisis of 2008, and ended following several years of designing, implementing, and testing business process controls in a mortgage business which initially could not charge fees at all for fear of regulatory noncompliance, a problem he helped resolve within a few months. From there he joined a healthcare distribution company weathering an unprecedented assault on its margins from self-distribution and the imminent entry of Amazon into its space. This afforded a front-row seat to a company's efforts to completely change its culture with the assistance of an outside consultant.

The guiding light in Veyera's career has been to find the most difficult business problems to solve and try to solve them. The repeated efforts to drive breakthrough improvements with Lean and Six Sigma—along with the realization that these were doomed to failure unless the companies' cultures were addressed—led to the book you're reading right now. It's the most difficult problem he could find and he's trying to help you solve it.

Veyera lives in Fort Lupton, CO, with his wife, Anita, his children Winston, Sophia, Christopher, and Clementine, two cats, and one dog. He is a graduate of the United States Air Force Academy and is proud to be '93.

Stay in Touch!

• • •

Email Jeff at jeff@engageconsulting.us

Follow Jeff and *Culture Is Everything* on Facebook: https://www.facebook.com /Culture-Is-Everything-104491954425804

Follow Jeff's YouTube Channel, CultureIsEverythingBook: https://www.youtube .com/channel/UC61G4eygGF19ij6zRqtxfkQ/

WHY ASQ?

ASQ is a global community of people passionate about quality, who use the tools, their ideas and expertise to make our world work better. ASQ: The Global Voice of Quality.

FOR INDIVIDUALS

Advance your career to the next level of excellence.

ASQ offers you access to the tools, techniques and insights that can help distinguish an ordinary career from an extraordinary one.

FOR ORGANIZATIONS

Your culture of quality begins here.

ASQ organizational membership provides the invaluable resources you need to concentrate on product, service and experiential quality and continuous improvement for powerful top-line and bottom-line results.

ASK A LIBRARIAN

Have questions? Looking for answers?
In need of information? Ask a librarian!

Customized research assistance from ASQ's research
librarian is one of the many benefits of membership.
ASQ's research librarian is available to answer
your research requests using the everexpanding
library of current and credible resources, including
journals, conference proceedings, case studies, and
Quality Press publications.

You can also contact the librarian to request permission
to reuse or reprint ASQ copyrighted material, such as
ASQ journal articles and Quality Press book excerpts.

**For more information or to submit a question,
visit asq.org/quality-resources/ask-a-librarian.**

TRAINING   CERTIFICATION   CONFERENCES   MEMBERSHIP   PUBLICATIONS